M000043130

Praise for *The Life of Mr. Baseball*

"Coach Cutler gives us a peek behind the curtain of the character of one of the winningest baseball coaches in Virginia history. I've known Coach for almost 40 years, and in his book, I got to relive our relationship and hear the stories of one of our unsung heroes who always served others with his heart and soul. In his words and in his kindness he will make you want to be a better person."

—Brian "Iron Ed" Hiner
Navy SEAL Lieutenant Commander (Ret.)
Author of *GUTS: Greatness Under Tremendous Stress*
Los Angeles Times Bestselling Author of *First, Fast, Fearless*

The Life of Mr. Baseball

Stories from Coach Cutler

by Jim Cutler

©2021 Joseph H. Cutler, Jr.

All rights reserved. No part of this book may be reproduced, stored
in a retrieval system, or transmitted in any form or by any means
(electronic, mechanical, photocopy, recording, or any other) except for
brief quotations in printed reviews, without prior permission in writing
from the publisher.

Cover illustration by Zim Jackson
Author photo by Brian Sennett

Interior book design by Naomi Middleton of Scribe Freelance
Cover design by Daniel Middleton of Scribe Freelance

ISBN: 978-0-9835435-4-1

List of Stories

Jim Cutler Timeline

1938   Born in Richlands, VA

1943   Started first grade in Baltimore, MD, age 5

1951–1952   Made 12 put outs at second base in one baseball game, Richlands High School

1953   Little League baseball coach, Richlands, age 15

1954   Tried out for the New York Yankees, summer after junior year of high school

1954–1955   Made 22 out of 26 free throws in one varsity basketball game, Richlands High School

1955   Graduation from Richlands High School, age 16

1955–1956   Greenbrier Military School, Lewisburg, WV

1956–1960   Hampden-Sydney College, Bachelor of Science Degree
Played football for Hampden-Sydney for 4 years, running back and kicker
Averaged 7 yards a carry for Hampden-Sydney College in varsity game against Bridgewater College
Played basketball for Hampden-Sydney for 1 year
Ran track for Hampden-Sydney for 1 year

1960–2007   Virginia Postgraduate Professional Teaching License in History, Mathematics, Spanish PreK-12, Government, General Science I

1960   Annual teaching salary was $3,250, Bedford County Public Schools

1960–2005   Teacher, Bedford High School (1960–64), Liberty High School (1964–2005), 45 years

1960–2006	Head baseball coach, Bedford High School, Liberty High School, 513 wins
1960–1964	Head j.v. football coach, Bedford High School, undefeated and unscored on season in 1962
1960–1992	Assistant football coach, Bedford High School, Liberty High School, 32 Years
1960–1964	Head boys j.v. basketball coach, Bedford High School
1960–1975	Officiated VHSL boys basketball, one year chosen by Blue Ridge District coaches to officiate tournament games at Salem Civic Center, officiated two games in one night (5:00 p.m. and 9:00 p.m.)
1965	University of Virginia, Master of Education Degree
1974–1982	Coached American Legion, Connie Mack, Little League, and Dixie League baseball
1976–1980	Head girls varsity basketball coach, Liberty High School, 67 wins and 17 losses
1977	Group AA VHSL Girls Basketball District, Regional Champions, 21-1
1978	Group AA VHSL Girls Basketball District, Regional Champions, 20-3
1978	Named Coach of the Year for Girls Basketball in the Seminole District
1977	Group AA VHSL Baseball District, Regional Champions, 23-4
1977	Group AA Virginia State Baseball Championship
1977	Grand Marshal of Christmas Parade in Bedford, VA
1978	Honored on the floor of the Virginia Assembly, House of Delegates
1981–1983	Assistant Wrestling Coach, Liberty High School
1986	Selected to coach baseball in the U.S. Olympic Festival, Houston, TX; players included Mike Mussina, Willie Banks, and Jesse Levis
1986	Ran four marathons in one year

1986	300th Career Win in Group AA VHSL Baseball
1990	Presented Quarter Century of Leadership & Devotion to Baseball Award by American Baseball Coaches Association
1995	400th Career Win in Group AA VHSL Baseball, first coach to achieve 400 wins
1996	Inducted into the Salem-Roanoke Baseball Hall of Fame
1996	Selected as Virginia's State Coach of the Year
1996	One of four finalists for National Coach of the Year
2001	Inducted into the Virginia High School League Hall of Fame
2001	Presented Key to City of Bedford
2002	Liberty High School Baseball Field named "Jim Cutler Field"
2003–2004	Golf Coach, Liberty High School, 2 years
2004	500th Career Win in Group AA VHSL Baseball
2005	Received 45 Year Career Award from the Virginia High School Coaches Association
2006	Retired from coaching baseball in Group AA VHSL with 513 victories and with 39 winning baseball seasons in 46 years, VHSL Seminole District Coach of the Year numerous times, VHSL All-Star Games coached several times
2014	Inducted into the Liberty High School Hall of Fame
2016	Made Honorary Navy SEAL by Retired Lieutenant Commander Navy SEAL Ed Hiner

Introduction

by Cherie Cutler Whitehurst

In August of 2020, my father, Jim Cutler, was diagnosed with stage 4 lung cancer. The diagnosis seemed unbelievable because my father was in better shape at over 80 than most 60-year-olds. He had spent a lifetime playing sports, coaching, running, and in later years biking and swimming. With this somber news, he remembered a project he had talked about many years ago with my mother: writing a book of stories about his life experiences. I encouraged him that this was a wonderful idea, as he has always been a great story teller, and I promised to help.

As my father began a new type of marathon, this book, he wrote with focus and speed. When he did not feel good, he would write. When he could not sleep, he would write. The stories began pouring out of him, and I found myself in the special place of reading these amazing stories first hand; they brought laughter, inspiration, and motivation.

Beginning in the fall of 2020, we settled into our routine of Dad writing the stories, reading them for me and answering questions that I had. I went to work typing each story as he completed them. Sometimes he preferred dictating the stories to me. One time he brought in several pieces of paper and told me the story, reading it off the papers. When it was time for him to leave, he gave me his notes, but there was not a single word written down! He had only pretended to be reading, and I fell for it completely. Fortunately, I was so captivated by what he was telling me that I remembered the whole story and had no trouble typing up his words.

We then continued for the next few months with him bringing me his stories or notes, me typing them out, and him cross-checking. It was a special gift for us. We would now like to share this gift of simple stories that reveal so much about the life of a one-of-a-kind man, a special husband, father, teacher, coach, community member, friend, and Christian from the generation born during the Great Depression.

"Coach"

Preface by Brian "Iron Ed" Hiner

Navy SEAL Lieutenant Commander (Ret.)

Author of *GUTS: Greatness Under Tremendous Stress* (April 2021)

Los Angeles Times Bestselling Author of *First, Fast, Fearless*

I grew up in the small town of Montvale, in the Blue Ridge Mountains of Virginia, with one class of fewer than 30 students in my grade. In the late 1970s, there wasn't much in Montvale, one small store and a gas station, and the world outside my town seemed big and scary to me. I grew up in poverty and a broken home filled with uncertainty and volatility, so I was a scared kid with little to no hope about my future. I wasn't a particularly good student; I was more worried about having electricity and food in my trailer when I came home from school. Fortunately for me, my life was about to change, and I was about to find my guiding light in an unforgettable coach.

When I graduated from seventh grade, my family had completely dissolved, and my brother and I moved in with our widowed grandmother to attend Liberty High School in Bedford, Virginia. Like many kids my age, I loved baseball, and I was obsessed with the game and the competition. Baseball became my thing, the one thing that I could do well, and it created the only dream I had at the time, to be a major league ballplayer. In my freshman year, I was determined to make the varsity baseball team and trained every day during the winter leading up to the tryouts. During these tryouts, I met the man I later realized would be one of the most influential people in my life, Coach Jim Cutler.

On the day of the final cuts, Coach pulled me into the locker room and explained the situation. I was only a freshman, so the parents were pressuring him to put me on the j.v. team and let their older sons have an opportunity that they felt I was taking from them. I broke down immediately and pleaded with him that this was all I had in my life, and it meant everything to me to make this team. Coach knew my situation at home and acted morally heroic, keeping me on varsity, knowing the parents would be angry, but he saw something in me, and I knew it, and knowing it has changed me forever. For the first time in my life, I could be someone who had something I could pursue. That season I was the triple-crown winner in hitting and one of the top winning pitchers.

After the season was over, Coach took me with his family to Myrtle Beach on my first family vacation and my first time seeing the ocean. Little did I know then that I would spend a lot of nights in the oceans of the world. I played four years under Coach Cutler's leadership, received a Division One scholarship and was fortunate enough to play at the Regional World Series level on two separate occasions. My dream of being a Major League Baseball player ended when my talent ran out, but thank God it did because I stumbled on what would be my future life's work: I met a Navy SEAL, and just like that, I found my calling.

I spent 20 years as a Navy SEAL and went from an enlisted SEAL to an Officer. I deployed on nine major deployments, three different wars, and before retiring, I was the Training Officer for all basic and advanced training for all Navy SEALs. Since retiring, I've become a best-selling author of *First, Fast, Fearless* and *GUTS* and even started an organization to train under-served children in mental toughness and resilience.

It's easy to look at our lives and blame the past or something other than ourselves for our shortcomings. But why do we not "blame" our success on our past or someone else? I could pat myself on the back all day as a self-made man, but that wouldn't be honest. Coach Cutler changed the trajectory of my life. He was a coach to me and a role model for being a good person, a father, and a husband. Everyone who knows him knows that he is a giver, not a taker.

He served his community and was one of the most successful coaches in Virginia history. More importantly, he gave kids like me hope and helped raise us as men on the baseball diamond, within the classroom, and in life. Coach's leading style is unique, and no player would ever say they were scared of Coach Cutler. But they would say they were terrified of letting him down or disappointing him because he didn't coach with fear; he coached with character. As a SEAL, I adopted Coach's style of leading: I didn't lead with fear, and I didn't focus on what people were doing wrong, but rather what they were doing right.

When I reflect back on my life, I must give gratitude to my coach not for just the things on the field but also for everything that he did to help a scared young kid from a tough background. I get tears in my eyes just writing this because I can feel the pain of that young kid crying in the locker room out of desperation and fear of his future. But then I can feel the love and caring that Coach Cutler gave a kid he barely knew, and those tears of fear turn to joy and appreciation.

Before you read his words, I hope you read mine to put Coach's nearly five decades of service to his community, family, and players into context. In my opinion, the word hero is often overused and given to those not deserving of the title. But as you read these stories, keep in mind that Coach Cutler *is* a hero to that scared and lonely kid crying in the locker room. And to me still. I wonder how many more young kids like me Coach Cutler influenced and shaped; my guess is a lot. So I'll take the liberty here and thank you, Coach, for everything you have done to change our lives forever.

HOOYAH Coach!

World War II

I was born in Richlands, Virginia, near the end of the Great Depression in 1938. At this time, living in Southwest Virginia was economically very difficult, and my family had to move to Baltimore, Maryland, at the start of WW II for my father to get work. My father found a job at Glenn L. Martin in Baltimore where they made airplanes for the U.S. government.

My earliest memories are watching the bombers fly over our home on their test flights before they were sent overseas to fight in the war effort. My friends and I would count the planes and then pretend with our fingers like we were shooting them down. One day, one of the bombers crashed in the woods close to my home.

I never played that game again with my friends.

The Glenn L. Martin plant was very important in the war effort and living close to it was dangerous. During the war there were blackout regulations which required that all windows and doors be covered at night with heavy curtains, cardboard, or paint so enemy aircraft would not be able to see our homes. Each night my family had to pull our blackout shades down so our home could not be seen from the air. It was a way of life and as a young child, I did not know any different.

The community in which we lived was made up of hard-working people who wanted to serve their country. When the war was over in 1945, the people were in the streets rejoicing. At the time, I did not understand what was happening. I asked my mother what was wrong and she said that the war was over. We were happy the terrible war was finished, but the jobs the people had were now gone and my father had to find work elsewhere. Soon after the war, my father loaded up his wife and his three small children and made the long journey back to Southwest Virginia to look for work and to enroll the children in school.

Mother

In the late 1940s my mother had become a public-school teacher in Cedar Bluff, Virginia. She was a good teacher and the students liked her because they said she cared about them. One time, however, she really showed me just how much she cared about my mouth. I was eight when I said some words that my mother did not like. I had heard the bad words at school and repeated them at home. My mother took a dish rag, put soap on it, and scrubbed my mouth with it. She told me never to use words like that again.

That day I learned a lesson that would affect me for the rest of my life. I never used profanity or vulgarity again. Over the years, I have been tempted, but I have tried to keep a clean mouth.

In addition my mother ensured I was in church every Sunday. My family attended the United Methodist Church in Richlands, Virginia. We never missed Sunday School and I sang in the church choir during the worship service.

My mother also had me take piano lessons. I still remember how one summer day I came home from playing in the neighborhood and found a large upright piano in our living room. Mother thought playing the piano would be good for me. For the next two years, I took piano lessons, which also meant I had to practice a half hour each day and had to perform in recitals. Even with just two years of lessons, today I still enjoy playing the piano at night and especially the old hymns.

While I would not recommend washing a child's mouth out with soap, I appreciate my mother's effort in the 1940s to instill goodness in me, but I much more appreciate her giving me a taste of the cultural arts.

Danger on the Bridge

When I was a young boy, I lived in the small town of Cedar Bluff in Southwest Virginia. My friends and I did not spend time indoors watching TV and playing video games. Instead, our days were spent playing on the bluffs along the Clinch River. To get to the bluffs, we had to cross the river by way of the railroad tracks. The Norfolk and Western Railroad ran from the coal fields of Southwest Virginia all the way to the Atlantic Ocean. It was a prosperous time for coal and I can remember seeing train engines pulling over 100 coal cars every day.

On our way to the bluffs we would have to make sure we were not on the bridge when a train was coming. We were foolish and had no idea what we were doing was even illegal. Furthermore, the deck truss bridge that went over the Clinch River also went over Route 460, and I am sure we could easily be seen from the road when we were on the bridge. I am surprised that no one reported us to our parents or law enforcement.

Many times, the boys in the town would put coins on the tracks so the trains would run over them. We would then collect the flattened coins and take them to school to show them off as a badge of honor. We knew what we were doing was dangerous but just how bad, we did not realize. To take precautions, we would put one of our ears down on the tracks to listen for any vibrations that would signal to us that a train was coming. When we felt sure there was no train, we would proceed onto the long bridge.

Several times, however, we were wrong about no train coming and had to run without falling to try to get across before the train came upon us. As young elementary age boys, we did not think about the train being unable to stop. There was one time in particular when I had a very close call: I had to run my fastest to get off the bridge before the train would run over me. It was after this incident that two of my friends were also caught on the bridge. They were not as fortunate as I was. They realized they were not going to be able to outrun the train and they ended up jumping off the bridge. The boys were seriously injured but lived. After this incident, I never played on the bridge again. My parents never knew we were playing on the bridge. They just thought we were playing in the country. Maybe TV and video games are not so bad after all.

Smokestack

One summer my family ended up with a very special pet, who not only became the talk of our town but also ended up protecting me. This pet was a very large black crow. You might ask, "How did you end up with a pet crow?" Well, it happened through the love and care my father gave it. My father loved nature and animals. If he saw a wounded animal, he would not just pass it by. He would try to help it. That is exactly what my father did for old Smokestack.

When my father found the big black crow on the ground injured, he picked up the bird and put him in a cage in the shade of our backyard. He took very good care of the crow making sure it had enough water and food each day. After several weeks, the crow began to look well so my father left the door to the cage open. To our surprise, the crow made his home with us. He would fly around our backyard but always return to his cage. The crow was unusually tame with the members of my family. He flew up to us and gently perched on our shoulders. My brother Tom, who spent a lot of time with him, called him Smokestack, and the name stuck.

This particular summer, I had started a new job as a paperboy delivering *The Roanoke Times* in Cedar Bluff, Virginia, where we lived. I was assigned a new route and told to build the number of my customers. I did as I was asked and increased my customer base by 100 people. The spike was so dramatic that the paper gave me a special award. I traveled the route in Cedar Bluff by bike for eight miles and made friends with everyone. People were particularly interested in Smokestack and loved watching him fly ahead of me and then ride on my handlebars. Every morning all summer he flew with me and at night he would go into his cage in the backyard. He was the talk of the town.

Some people think that crows liking shiny things is just a myth, but I have to tell you that Smokestack was always bringing us gifts of "shiny things" he found during the day. He brought back jewelry, coins and keys to his cage. Smokestack was *so* obsessed with bringing us "shiny things" that he flew into people's yards and parked cars/homes with open windows to grab the items he spied. Once a week my brother, sister, and I had the chore of going throughout the neighborhood seeing if any of the "shiny things" belonged to the neighbors, and making sure they got their items back. While at first the crow was cute on my bike, Smokestack became an irritation to some of the people he had taken the "shiny things" from. They did not laugh as much when they saw what Smokestack had taken from them.

While I sometimes wondered if my bird brought the "shiny things" as gifts because he cared for us or just because he liked them, I was made to know for certain that he cared for me when I was attacked one day while I was delivering the papers. One of the families that got the paper had chickens and a banty rooster. This rooster was aggressive and mean. Every time I delivered the paper to this family, it chased me and I had to run fast from it. Several times the rooster jumped up on my leg and even drew blood. I had become scared of that "bird" and dreaded delivering the paper to this house.

One day, however, my crow was with me. As soon as Smokestack saw the rooster chasing me, he immediately flew after the mean banty rooster with no fear. Feathers flew everywhere and my crow emerged from the dust. From that time on that banty rooster never ever came after me. Smokestack had taught that banty rooster a lesson and protected me.

Late in the summer my crow disappeared and never returned. I hoped Smokestack had started a family, but we never saw him again. Today, I have a picture of a crow on a wall in my home. When I look at the picture, I remember the "shiny gifts" and the protection Smokestack gave me when I was chased by that mean banty rooster.

Coal Country

Growing up in Southwest Virginia, I was around coal most of my life. When I was a boy, I shared a bedroom with my brother Tom, who was two years younger. We had a coal furnace in the house and my job was to keep coal in it during the winter time. If the house got cold, then it was most obvious that my chores had not been done.

When I was in high school, I had the opportunity to work with coal. My neighbor was a supervisor in a nearby coal tipple in Buchanan County, Virginia. He asked me if I would like to have a job where he worked. He said I would be able to ride with him each day. Needless to say, I took the job and it was a great experience.

My job at the coal tipple was to weigh the coal trucks that brought their coal there. All the trucks had been weighed previously without their loads of coal. When the trucks drove on the scales at my station, I had the task of weighing the trucks with their loads, writing the weight down, and writing the number assigned to identify the coal truck. Afterward the trucks proceeded to where the coal was sorted and the coal was loaded on the train cars. During training, my supervisor emphasized how important it was to be 100 percent accurate with collecting my records, which tied to the livelihood for the coal truck drivers. In other words, the drivers' pay was based on the amount of coal they hauled away from the coal mines and to the coal tipple.

During my time on this job, I only had one issue. One morning we were late getting to the coal tipple and there were already almost 70 trucks lined up to be weighed. As you might guess, the coal truck drivers were not very happy that morning. Fortunately, I was driving in with the boss so I was in the clear.

My roots in coal country go back to my grandfather, Isaac Cleveland Boyd. He was the grandson of a Methodist Episcopal minister, Isaac Newton Boyd, Jr., and the son of the Treasurer of Buchanan County, Virginia, Elihu Kiser Boyd. My grandfather was a school teacher, businessman, grocery store owner, House Delegate for the Virginia General Assembly representing Russell County, and the owner of a small coal company. He served in the General Assembly as a young man in the 1920s and then returned to serve again later in life. When he ran in 1941 as a Democrat, the slogan on his campaign card was, "A Man With the Experience of Two Previous Terms."

With several of his daughters being school teachers and himself being a former teacher, my grandfather served on the Schools and Colleges Committee and on a committee for Mining and Mineral Resources.

My grandfather became interested in coal when he ended up with quite a bit of land during the Depression. When people could not pay their bills at his grocery store, he would allow them to trade for a piece of property. After the Depression he continued to purchase land, accumulating around 5,000 acres in Buchanan and Russell Counties. Much of this land was mountainous and had some minerals on it.

As time went on, my grandfather leased his properties to several coal companies. They would pay him about 10 cents a ton for the coal they mined off his property. Unfortunately, the big coal corporations took advantage of the small business landowners and my grandfather had to always be watching their work. He was known to go to the mines often and count the coal trucks coming out, making sure the number of trucks matched what he was paid.

The family, however, never ended up rich. One reason was because the coal corporations had put an anti-inflation clause into the contract with my grandfather. When the coal business began to prosper, the price remained capped at a ridiculously low amount per ton for the coal. This same injustice happened to others who had anti-inflation clauses written into their contracts.

For years after my grandfather passed, his daughters ran his company but never obtained much money. After the sisters died, their children then began serving on the Board of Directors. As one of the eldest cousins, I served on the Board of Directors for 15 years and as the Vice Chairman of the Board for a period. In recent years, I have stepped aside giving the opportunity to some of the younger cousins to serve.

Never Too Small

As a young man growing up in Richlands, Virginia, I dreamed of playing football for the Blue Tornadoes. The Richlands High School football team was an outstanding ball team and had a coach named Ernie Hicks. He had coached for many years and was considered one of the best coaches in Southwest Virginia. I had played junior varsity football for two years and was ready to fulfill my dream of playing for Coach Hicks on the varsity team. I was 5'7" tall and weighed 135 lbs., but I was quick and I could kick.

In August, we had a team meeting to get our uniforms. We were all excited to start practice. Uniforms were given out to the 35 young men and Coach Hicks asked if he had left anyone out. I had not received my uniform so I raised my hand. Coach Hicks looked at me, and in front of all my friends he said, "You are too small to play for Richlands; you might get hurt."

I left the locker room in tears as my friends suited up for practice. Coach Hicks was not giving me a chance to show him what I could do. My best friend Sandy Robinson later consoled me and said, "Don't give up. You will get your chance later." This encouragement meant a lot to me. After getting over the disappointment of not making the team, I became more motivated to show the coach he was wrong, and continued to work out.

Two weeks later, Coach Hicks came to me and said he heard that I was a kicker and asked me if I would like to join the team as a kicker. For the next two years, I played for the Richlands Blue Tornadoes varsity football team and was able to fulfill my dream. As a kicker, I was known for accuracy and performance under pressure. In the community and in the local paper I was known as "Golden Toe Cutler" who never missed. What Coach Hicks told me about my size affected my life, but in a positive way. I learned to work even harder and to never quit.

After graduating from Richlands High School, I attended Hampden-Sydney College and played varsity football for all my four years there. And after college, I became a teacher and a coach. In all my 46 years of coaching, I remembered never to judge an athlete by his or her size. Instead, I looked at an athlete's heart and skills.

After coaching for four years at Bedford High School and then 41 years at Liberty High School, I was inducted into the Virginia High School League (VHSL) Hall of Fame in Charlottesville, Virginia. It was several years after my induction that I learned that Coach Hicks had not been inducted into the VHSL Hall of Fame to honor him for his many years of outstanding service.

Coach Hicks began his coaching career in 1924 and retired in 1963. During those 39 years, Coach Hicks took one year off, 1943-1944, to serve his country in the armed services during World War II. During his career, he led the Richlands High School Football team to 167 wins, and during the 1950s he led a winning streak of 64 wins with thirty losses and one tie. During his tenure, his team won two District VII championships, one area championship, and one regional championship. The football stadium at Richlands High School bears his name, as the Ernie Hicks Stadium.

I learned that community members had tried to have Coach Hicks inducted into the VHSL Hall of Fame, but were unsuccessful. I then joined their fight, and so years after Coach Hicks had retired and passed away, I had the distinct privilege of helping Coach Hicks be inducted into the VHSL Hall of Fame. Today, in 2021, Coach Hicks' Hall of Fame plaque hangs next to mine in the VHSL office in Charlottesville, Virginia.

Coming to Faith

When I was about 14, there was a tent revival on one of the ball fields right behind the Baptist Church. I had come to the revival on my own. I cannot tell you how I got to the revival or even why I was there. What's important is that I was there.

At the end of the service, there was an altar call and by myself I walked down the long aisle in the big tent filled with people. I had a strange feeling that came over me as I walked down front. I accepted Jesus as my Savior, committed my life to Him, and received God's grace. From this point, I made it a habit to read my Bible and an Upper Room devotional each evening and pray. Throughout my life, God has always been with me providing me with strength and a lot of forgiveness: like the one time when I kicked dirt at an umpire. By no means have I led a perfect life, and that is especially why I am grateful for God's grace in Jesus Christ.

Over the years, I have been successful and I thank God for all of His blessings. There have been times when life has been hard, and that was when I had to learn to put my faith in God and trust Him.

John Wesley said, "Best of all, God is with us."

God has been with me.

The Double-Blind Date

I met my wife Justine in college when we were on a double-blind date. Her date, whose name I will not mention and who happened to be a good friend of mine, had gotten stone drunk.

I had grown up around aunts and uncles who drank a great deal of alcohol and I had seen first-hand the serious dangers of alcoholism. I knew better than to drink on a date. Not drinking during this particular date, however, really paid off because I ended up with the girls. I took care of Justine and kept up with my own date too.

Justine and I soon started seeing more of each other and we began to date on a regular basis. She would come to all my dances and social events at Hampden-Sydney College and I would go to all her dances and social events at Longwood College. She would also come to all my sporting events at Hampden-Sydney. I could always count on her being in the stands cheering for me.

At Hampden-Sydney I played on the football team for all four years. I was one of the team's running backs and the kicker. I was involved in a variety of other sports at the college level as well such as basketball and baseball. One year I even participated in track and field. Justine was in the stands when I had a pole-vaulting accident and ended up with my face purple and blue from the bruises. She had no problem still walking down the street with me even though my face was severely bruised and swollen. She never judged me and always showed me support, even when I did not do as good.

I gave Justine my fraternity pin my sophomore year and we were engaged at Christmas our senior year. We were married on December 22, 1960. In my 46 years of coaching, she only missed one game, and that was due to her receiving a chemotherapy treatment for cancer.

My "Big" Younger Brother

My brother Tom is two years younger than I am, but at 6'1", he is six inches taller. In high school he was an outstanding basketball and track athlete. After graduating from high school he attended Lynchburg College and competed in cross-country and track and field. The fall of his freshman year he had a great cross-country season. In the spring, he ran track and field and competed in the one-mile and two-mile races, winning almost all of them. During Tom's freshman year, I was a senior at Hampden-Sydney College. I had the opportunity to drive to Lynchburg College to see Tom run in the state meet his freshman year. He came in third in the one-mile race as a college freshman. I was really impressed. I thought by the time he was a senior, he would easily come in first. Little did I know that I was watching Tom run the one-mile race for the very last time.

In November of 1960, Tom's sophomore year, he went deer hunting with my father and several other men in Bath County, Virginia. Before sunrise, as the group was walking deep in the woods towards their deer stand using their flashlights, the group was shot at and Tom's leg was hit. He was shot by a hunter in another group who thought Tom was a deer. Tom was carried out of the woods by his father and the other men. Four hours later, Tom arrived at Roanoke Memorial Hospital.

At that time, I was teaching at Bedford High School as a first-year teacher. As soon as I received word that Tom had been shot, I drove to Roanoke Memorial to be with him, my father, my mother, and my sister. When I got to the hospital, Tom was unconscious, and was taken into surgery. The doctors told the family that so much damage was done to the leg that it had to be amputated. In addition, they thought Tom was suffering kidney damage. As a result, Tom was taken by ambulance to the University of Virginia

Hospital in Charlottesville, which was 119 miles away. The doctors at UVA confirmed what we had been told by the doctors at Roanoke Memorial: Tom's leg had to be amputated above the knee. Tom's life was saved, but he was destined to live as an amputee the rest of his life.

While the accident had a profound effect on my family, my brother refused to see himself as someone with a disability and sought to live life as independently and as normally as possible. After Tom had been fitted for his prosthesis, the doctor told him they would now help him return to school. Tom, however, informed the doctor that he had already been back at school and in his classes using his crutches to go up and down the stairs.

He went on to graduate from Lynchburg College with a Bachelor of Science degree and the University of Virginia with a Master of Education degree. Tom married a beautiful bride, Louise, and had two great children, Chris and Betsy Ann. He taught school in the Lynchburg area for close to 40 years. Whenever I ran into his former students or teachers who worked with my brother, they always commented to me how encouraging he was and what a fun sense of humor he had. Several of his students expressed that he was a positive influence in their lives.

Since that November day in 1960, Tom has remained an outdoorsman, hunting and fishing. He has been an inspiration to his family, and to his many friends. Today he lives with his wife in Elon, Virginia, and will always be my courageous "big" younger brother.

Church

When my wife, Justine, and I came to live and work in Bedford, Virginia, we joined Main Street United Methodist Church. Justine and her family had been members of Belmont United Methodist Church in Roanoke, Virginia, and my family and I had been members of First United Methodist Church in Richlands. So, it was only natural that we would begin our married life at the United Methodist Church in Bedford.

As a young married couple, we were the counselors of the United Methodist Youth Fellowship (UMYF) group. At the time in Bedford, we also had a Town Youth Group that was made up of many different churches. Justine and I also supported this group in leadership and chaperoning. Through the years, she and I continued to be very active at Main Street. I took on positions such as Lay Leader, Chairman of the Pastor Parish Relations Committee, Chairman of the Administrative Board, member of the choir, and Board of Trustees Member. I also participated in Lay Witness Missions and was active in the Walk to Emmaus program. Most importantly, Justine and I made it a priority to have our four children in Sunday School and church each Sunday, when at times this was not easy.

The Marbles

As I was a new teacher at Bedford High School, I was just a couple of years older than the students. While I did not have classroom management problems, I had to think creatively.

In addition to teaching, one of my duties was to take a turn supervising over 35 students in a study hall, held in the auditorium of Bedford High School. The floors were wooden and like most auditoria, they sloped. The chairs were also wooden and the ceilings very high. As a result, the acoustics in the auditorium were extremely loud. Everything that dropped, moved, or rolled could be heard as a blaring echo.

There were about six boys who liked to sit in the back of the auditorium. When no one was looking, this mischievous sextet liked to roll marbles down the sloped floor during the study hall. As the balls rolled, they picked up speed echoing louder and louder. To make matters worse, when one of the marbles rolled on a young girl's shoe, the snickering grew even more. In just a matter of seconds a teacher could easily lose control of his or her class.

The teachers were beside themselves when it was their turn to supervise the study hall because of these boys, complaining to the principal and demanding that he take disciplinary action. When it was my turn to supervise, however, I did not have the discipline problems and the other teachers could not understand why.

Here was my secret:

At the beginning of the study hall period, I would stand at the entrance collecting all the marbles out of the students' pockets before they were allowed to come in and sit down. I also required the six boys to sit on the front row of the auditorium. The students were then in their seats before the tardy bell rang and were on task the entire period.

After school, however, and before football practice, I would take the group of six out into the courtyard next to the auditorium. There, they were able to play a real game. I returned all the marbles to them that I had collected and got them in formation to play. The boys would see how many marbles they could knock out while others watched. The group began to look forward to this activity and students in my study hall were always well-behaved. In this instance, being able to think creatively and like a teenager really came in handy.

The Miracle of Plastic Surgery

Justine and I were married in December of 1960. In June of 1962 our first child, Cherie Anne, made the scene. Like most new parents, we were so excited to have our first child. The labor for Justine had been long, nearly 24 hours, and then I was finally able to see Justine and meet our new daughter. Just before I met Cherie, Justine told me that everything was all right but there was a little birthmark on the left side of Cherie's face and several birthmarks on the top and left side of her head. When I first saw Cherie, the birthmarks were barely noticeable, but as the days passed, the little birthmark on the left side of her face began to grow extremely large. The birthmark soon covered almost the entire left side of her face, from her nose to her ear and from just below her eye to almost the bottom of her face.

The birthmark was called a hemangioma, a vascular tumor. There are some hemangioma types that are flat and under the skin. Other types are raised and are above the skin. Some hemangiomas fade away in time, but other types of hemangiomas will not fade and can become serious as they grow. Cherie's type was growing out of control and there was concern that her left eye, nose, and mouth could soon be impacted by it. The specialists had recommended that the hemangiomas, particularly the one on the left side of her face, be radiated to slow down the growth.

The hemangiomas on the top and left side of her head responded to the radiation, but the hemangioma on the left side of her face was unresponsive and continued to grow. After several more radiation treatments, we learned that our daughter had been given too much radiation and the hemangioma on her face had become infected and was extremely painful for her. She cried a lot and we did not know how to console her. To make matters worse, her arms had to be put in splints so she would not pull on her face.

We tried to lead a normal life and keep active, but people were cruel sometimes. When people saw our daughter, they could not help but stare and then point and ask questions like, "What is that thing on her face?" Some people were even afraid of her thinking she had some type of contagious disease. Cherie's disfigurement became so disruptive we started staying away from public places. At one point, we felt like we could not even take her to church and have her in the nursery. We were at a loss as to what to do because the tumor continued to spread. One measurement of the mass that I remember was two inches by three inches, which was large, especially for an infant.

As Cherie turned a year old, some of the doctors knew we needed to look at immediate surgery to try to remove the vascular tumor. The thought was to remove the mass and take skin from her hip to graft into the area. These doctors had prepared us to expect, following the surgery, paralysis and severe drooping on the left side of her face due to their having to cut the seventh nerve. There were other doctors, however, that thought the surgery should not even be attempted and we should do nothing and maybe think about the surgery when she was a teenager. These days were very difficult. We were watching our little girl deal with the overdose of radiation that had ulcerated her face and caused infection, and our team of doctors could not agree on what exactly needed to be done.

My mother, Alice Cutler, who at this time was a teacher in Roanoke City, became very involved in Cherie's situation. She began researching the condition and most specifically who would be the best surgeon for her. My mother's search led her to a surgeon at the Medical College of Virginia (MCV), Dr. Leroy Smith, one of the top plastic surgeons in the United States.

Dr. Smith was born in 1913 with a cleft lip and cleft palate. He was operated on at six weeks of age, at one year of age, and numerous other times until he was 16. In 1942 he received his board certification for general surgery and practiced in Richmond, Virginia, and in 1950, he was one of the very first to receive certification in the area of plastic surgery by the American Board of Plastic Surgery. From this point on, plastic surgery became his focus. I have to believe that it was because of his own experience that he went into the medical field becoming a general surgeon and then a plastic surgeon. As the only active board-certified plastic surgeon in Richmond, Dr. Smith helped spearhead a professorship in pediatric plastic surgery at MCV.

When we met Dr. Smith, we saw that he was unlike any of the other doctors. To our amazement, he immediately picked Cherie up and kissed her. We saw how he treated her like a normal child, and we could sense his care for her. As he held Cherie in his arms and looked at her, he said, "I can help her. I can do the surgery in the next few weeks; she will also need to have several additional operations in the years to come."

We had finally found our doctor and we knew that Cherie was in good hands. So, at one and a half years of age, Cherie had her first surgery at MCV. After what seemed like hours in surgery, Dr. Smith appeared outside the operating room. We noticed he had tears in his eyes. He said, "She is going to be beautiful. Now she will be able to be a part of many activities as she grows up."

A miracle had happened. As Dr. Smith was operating, he found he would not have to do the skin graft. Instead, after he cut out the mass and most of the flesh of her cheek to get to the roots, he was able to stretch her skin from her left ear all the way over to her nose and mouth. He stitched along her nose and mouth and also under her eye. The skin graft was therefore not needed and there was hardly any paralysis. There were, of course, many surgeries and more times of Cherie being restrained in arm splints as a toddler and three-year-old, but she took it in stride. Her surgeries continued into her upper elementary and junior high school years. I am not sure exactly how many surgeries there were, but I believe at one point I counted seven.

As Cherie grew, she participated in many activities and loved being with people. There were a few incidents where she was called names in elementary school such as "scar face" and made fun of in junior high school, like the boy who told her in front of the other kids, "It looks like you cried a tear of acid," but she overcame the bullying and did not let it stop her. With each surgery, the scarring became less noticeable and her mother bought her a special make-up that was designed to cover scars.

Cherie especially liked studying ballet and piano and enjoyed entering and winning piano competitions. She started playing varsity basketball in the tenth grade and was the first girl to play on the Liberty High School golf team. During the fall seasons, she was a cheerleader for Liberty High School. She participated in Sunday School, sang in the choir, and was a member of the United Methodist Youth Fellowship (UMYF). She was even selected to play a lead role as Ado Annie in the musical *Oklahoma*, which was directed by her mother, and performed three times to a sellout crowd in the Liberty High School auditorium. To our amazement, her senior year she was selected as the Liberty High School Homecoming Queen for the Class of 1980. As she stood with the roses in her arms and the crown on her head, her mother and I felt like God was giving us and her an extra special blessing.

Cherie went on to graduate from James Madison University, and became a teacher and even coached a girls' basketball team which lost only one game. In 1995, she was selected as the Bedford County Public Schools Teacher of the Year and later became an assistant principal. She also earned a doctorate from Virginia Tech in 2004. In 2000 she became the head principal of Staunton River High School. After leading Staunton River High School for six years, she became the principal of Liberty High School in 2006, where she had graduated from high school. In 2009, she became the Assistant Superintendent for Bedford County Public Schools, later renamed the Deputy Superintendent.

During her career, she worked hard to ensure every young person received a quality education and reached their full potential. She was known in the Bedford community as an administrator who could turn challenged schools around to have much higher student achievement, better school discipline, and a more positive and caring school culture. Cherie supported her teachers and worked hard to build extra-curricular programs. She stood up to bullies and would not put up with students, adults, or groups of people being bullied or treated in a demeaning manner to their faces, behind their backs, or through inappropriate actions.

Cherie stood for truth, respect, dignity, and equality for all people, and I will always be proud of her. Without Dr. Leroy Smith, I do not believe Cherie would have been able to lead the life she has lived, nor had the opportunity to impact as many people in such a positive way. I will always be grateful to God for making the miracle of plastic surgery happen, and for how God used the hands and heart of Dr. Leroy Smith.

Moonshine

I began teaching at Bedford High School in Bedford, Virginia, in 1960. In the fall of 1964, Liberty High School opened, consolidating several community schools such as Big Island High School, Montvale High School, Boonsboro High School, New London Academy, and Bedford High School. I went from teaching very small classes to classes of over 30 students. I believe the cap for enrollment in a teacher's class was based on how many desks the principal could fit in the room, and my room was maxed to capacity with student desks.

On one of the first days of school at Liberty High School, I had met a large and strong looking young man who was in one of my government classes. I will call him Sam for purposes of this story. Sam was over six feet tall, weighed at least 250 pounds, and wore bib overalls. Privately, before school that first week, I had talked to him about coming out for our football team. He had thought about it and had politely said, "No, I am needed too much to work on my family's farm." I certainly respected his need to help his family but was disappointed for him to miss the experience of being a part of a team.

Just a few days later we were in class. I had taken roll, gone over the announcements, and was walking around checking to ensure the students had their new textbooks and materials. All of a sudden, a girl with a very pretty white sweater jumped out of her seat, started screaming, and ran out of the classroom as fast as she could with one of her friends following her. A terrible odor floated through the classroom. The students quietly filed out of the classroom and went into the hallway, but Sam was in his seat with his head down and vomit was all around him. Apparently, he had projected the vomit with such force that it went all over the back of the girl's white sweater.

I went over to Sam and tried to rouse him, but could not.

The assistant principal and principal were called along with an ambulance. About 15 minutes later, the ambulance arrived. The EMTs had trouble getting a pulse on Sam and the situation was most serious. One of the EMTs then notified me that he thought Sam had been drinking. The administration went to work to find out what Sam had consumed. We soon learned that earlier that morning Sam had gone into the boys' bathroom and several students had dared him to drink half a jug of moonshine that had been brewed on a local mountain.

Sam was rushed to the hospital still unconscious. In fact, Sam remained unconscious for hours. He lived but he was expelled from school. I never saw Sam again.

I had hoped that Sam would find a way to graduate through summer school, but I never heard. I hope life was good to him. I never forgot him in my 45 years of teaching.

The Reenactment of the Battle of Bunker Hill

My first year teaching at Liberty High School I had a wonderful group of students who later became good friends throughout the years. Several of my ball players were in my fifth period American History class. We were studying the Revolutionary War and the students were presenting their group projects. Some of the groups included young men such as Joe Heller, Watts Key, Jimmy Whorley, Lloyd Goode, and David Bradley. These students were very active learners and enjoyed their class projects. They reenacted the Battle of Bunker Hill, one of the key battles of the Revolutionary War, and played their roles sincerely. They had the room rearranged and were very loud with their sound effects, especially when it came to the artillery going off.

The teacher down the hall came down to my classroom and saw this group of students giving their presentation, which partially involved their acting out the battle. Instead of talking to me, she went to the principal to complain.

As soon as the presentation was over, the students returned to their desks and started their reading. The principal, William Lee, then walked into my classroom. He saw the students behaving as model students.

I said, "Mr. Lee, may I help you, sir?"

"I just came down to check on you," he replied, scanning the now silent room.

It was a great class as they learned about the Revolutionary War.

Who said learning can't be fun?

Double Trouble and Double Blessings

It was the summer of 1965, and my wife, Justine, was expecting our second child due in August. In those days, doctors did not perform ultrasounds, and expecting parents knew very little about their babies.

Justine had a typical pregnancy, except for the fact that she became very large *fast*. In the 1960s in Bedford County, female teachers were not allowed to continue teaching when their pregnancies became obvious. Teachers at this time made very little money and it took two salaries to afford a small three-bedroom house. Because we were so strapped for money, Justine had tried to conceal her pregnancy. Instead of wearing maternity clothes, she wore size 18 women's clothes. There came the day, however, when her pregnancy was discovered and she was made to stop teaching. We were just grateful that she was able to teach a few extra months due to her ingenious way of concealing her condition.

It was on a summer day in 1965 when we finally learned why Justine had become so large. Justine had been at the doctor and I was waiting for her as I lay in the sunshine in her parents' backyard. In those days they did not want the fathers in the doctor's office. Justine entered the backyard with a smile on her lips. The doctor had just x-rayed her stomach to find out the position of the baby, but had learned more than the position. She smiled and told me, "There are two of them."

I was at a loss for words. I was more than excited and pleased, but shocked. We should have seen the signs. Twins were on Justine's Blount side of the family, and on our wedding day, Justine had cracked a double yoked egg to fry that she forgot to tell me about. Needless to say, we were ecstatic and thankful for our double blessing.

Kenneth Holden and Michael Wade were born right on time but were both breech, which meant a very hard labor and delivery for Justine. The twins turned out to be identical and were considered mirror twins in that Ken was left-handed and Mike was right-handed. They were both very small at first and had to spend some time in an incubator but they soon began to thrive.

In raising twins, there was never a dull moment. Even though we stayed tired, we had to be alert at all times ensuring the boys were fed as needed. One time, we made the mistake of feeding one of the twins twice and not feeding the other. We ended up with both boys crying with great intensity, one with hunger and the other with a tummy ache.

The twins, for some reason, took their time learning to talk. Justine and I believed they took their time because at first, they had their own special language. We heard and saw them clearly communicating and talking to each other, but we had no idea what they were actually saying.

We also knew early on that the boys were going to be competitors. Instead of just crying when they wanted something, they would drop to the floor and begin banging their heads on the ground. It was almost as if they were trying to outdo each other. Justine and I were so concerned about their banging their heads on the floor that we made an appointment to see their doctor. To our surprise, the doctor advised us to ignore them and to just let them bang their heads. "Don't worry," the doctor said, "they will stop when it hurts."

Nevertheless, their head banging only continued. This was especially problematic when we would go to church and take them to the nursery. When Justine and I would leave, their crying and head banging would start up. The nursery workers were petrified. Finally, I had enough and bought them both football helmets they could wear to the church nursery. The helmets worked for a while, but then the twins learned to take their helmets off and still bang their heads. Thank God, somehow, they finally outgrew banging their brains on the ground and learned to use their words.

We also knew early on that the twins were going to be mischievous. After they began sitting at the table and were required to eat the food on their plates, Justine found their stash of scrambled eggs behind the refrigerator that had collected. This sneakiness continued into their high school years as they would switch schedules and attend the other brother's classes. And even switch dates with each other.

We taught the twins discipline as best we could, however, even this was difficult. One time when one of the twin's misbehaved, I spanked the wrong twin as Justine had accidentally directed. The other one thought it was extremely funny. That one then had to be disciplined.

Both boys grew up to be fine young men. They earned Bachelor of Science degrees from Radford University in Physical Education and have beautiful families of their own. Justine and I were always very proud of them and grateful for the double blessing.

My Third Son

"The doctor is not here yet. Stop the baby from coming. Knock her out!" These were the words my wife, Justine, heard as she was being put to sleep, before our fourth child was born.

It was only 13 months after our twin boys were born that Jeffrey Boyd came into the world. He was a perfect baby. He did not cry much. He was content, happy, good natured, and slept a lot. Having a baby just 13 months behind twins was almost like having triplets. I was thrilled and could only imagine having the opportunity to coach all three of the boys someday on a baseball team.

Jeff grew up loving baseballs, basketballs, and footballs. He kept up with his twin brothers and was very coordinated. When he finished the third grade, however, we sensed something was wrong. He was not progressing with his reading as he should have. We took him to many specialists and then we finally learned that Jeff was legally blind in one of his eyes. He was able to see light and that was about it. Through his excellent coordination, however, the problem had been masked. In addition, Jeff possessed a high ability level, but after the third grade, his achievement was not in keeping with his ability level. Reading was hard for Jeff. Justine and I were both teachers and yet we did not have the specialized skills that it took to help him work around his challenges.

These were the days before school districts were required by law to serve students with disabilities. As a result, to provide Jeff with the specialized instruction he needed, we sent him to the Achievement Center in Roanoke, Virginia. It was there that Jeff learned to read. The specialized educators at the Achievement Center knew how to help Jeff compensate for the blindness in his eye and allow his achievement to better match his ability level.

They identified Jeff as a kinesthetic learner, one who learned best by doing. As a result, the educators at the center pumped in as much information into his mind kinesthetically, as opposed to visually. While learning for him was not easy, he finally knew how to read. The disability did not go away, but he learned to work around it.

In time, Jeff was finally able to make his way back into the regular classroom in a regular school. He graduated from Liberty High School, and did end up playing on the LHS baseball team with his older brothers. He also went on to become an EMT and paramedic. His organizational skills and attention to detail became a strength.

What caused this disability is not known, but my wife wondered if there was some oxygen deprivation because the nurses delayed his birth until a doctor arrived. We will never know but are grateful that Jeff had the help he did before it was too late. My wife and I were teachers, and we still had trouble ensuring that Jeff received the educational services that he needed to succeed. I have to wonder how many other children born into this era did not get the education they required before it was too late. It is sad to think about.

A Nightmare and A Miracle

I grew up in Southwest Virginia in the 1950s. Every summer my parents, Alice and Joe Cutler, would take the family on a two-week vacation. Usually, we would head to the East Coast. We enjoyed the beach where we could fish and play in the ocean.

When Justine and I were married and had children, my mother and father continued the tradition of going on a summer vacation, now not with just their children, but also with their children's spouses and children too. One of these vacations, however, turned out to be a nightmare.

But also a miracle.

In August of 1967, my daughter, Cherie, had just turned five years old. My twin sons, Mike and Ken, were two and Jeff was almost one. My mother and father arranged for the whole family to have a vacation at Yaupon Beach, North Carolina. We saved all year so we could be together. Trying to economize we stayed in a motel across the street from the ocean. During the trip my wife, Justine, had confided in my mother that she had an uneasy feeling that she could not shake. Justine was a strong Christian woman who turned to God and prayed fervently when distressed.

It was our third day on our vacation, and I decided to take twins Mike and Ken to the beach for a late afternoon time to play in the sand. I pushed them in their double stroller across the highway that had a speed limit of 25 mph. Just as we made it across, I heard a little voice coming toward me saying, "Daddy, wait on me. I want to go too."

The next few minutes were a blur. Cherie was trying her best to get to me as fast as she could and in her effort had run in front of a car that was speeding. The young teenage male driver had just washed his car and was driving unusually fast and in his own words said, "I was driving fast to dry off the car."

Fortunately, the young driver had seen her, applied his brakes, but was too late. His car hit Cherie. She was knocked on the hood of the car and then up against the front windshield before she flew through the air landing on the asphalt road. Time stood still as I saw her lying beside the car on the hot road.

People ran over to us from everywhere. Justine came running from the motel. It was not a good sight. An ambulance was called, but had to travel from a town 10 miles away. Someone brought a thick woolly blanket and laid it on Cherie. A woman in a blue and white scarf with dark hair, whom we did not know, knelt down beside Cherie and in a loud and authoritative voice kept telling her, "You are going to be all right."

Finally, the ambulance arrived. Cherie was a very brave little girl as they loaded her onto the stretcher and into the ambulance. Justine and I both climbed into the ambulance with her. The sirens quickly began to blow loudly and the ambulance went faster than I have ever traveled by vehicle, going so fast that Justine and I were thrown around in the back. For everyone's safety, I had to tell the driver to slow down. For Cherie, however, she did not notice the high speed. She was extremely peaceful as she looked out the window commenting on how beautiful the colors were.

Our nightmare was that Cherie was hit by a car. Our miracle was that she survived. While she was seriously bruised and scraped, no bones were broken. Her head, however, hurt very much; it was hard for her to even lay it on her pillow in the hospital. Cherie was bruised all over and her whole left arm and side were scabbed. She was not able to enjoy the rest of our time at the beach or get back in the ocean.

After my daughter came home from the hospital my mother comforted my wife by saying, "Well, now it is over. You can relax." My wife's uneasy feeling that she had told my mother about was no doubt a message from God to pray. When you get those uneasy feelings, pray.

Running the Whitewater Rapids on the James River

Several years after my brother Tom and I had graduated from college and begun our teaching careers, he purchased a 10-foot-long canoe and wanted me to go fishing with him. Our plan was to put the canoe in the water where the Maury River meets the James River, which is several miles below Glasgow, Virginia, and 12 miles north of Big Island. We would float down the James in the canoe fishing for smallmouth bass. After a time of fishing and relaxing, we would then drive Tom's pickup truck back to my car where we had launched.

We loaded our fishing poles and a cooler filled with drinks and sandwiches into the canoe. I was in the front with a paddle and Tom was in the back with one as well. It was a beautiful day and we were soon on our way down the James River fishing. The fish were biting and we caught several smallmouth. We were pretty pleased to be catching the fish so easily, but when Tom caught a citation fish that was 18 inches in length, we were very pleased.

The James River runs between two Blue Ridge Mountain gaps that are about 3,000 feet in elevation. The view was beautiful as we floated down the river looking up to the top of the mountains. It had rained upstream the night before so the river was running fast. It seemed like no time until Tom and I could hear and see the whitewater we were headed towards.

Over the years, the river had formed rapids called Balcony Falls, a run that was made up of mostly Class II rapids but was also an easy Class III in some sections. Even today people come from miles away to experience them. They say this is perfect whitewater for beginners, yet these rapids also keep the interest of intermediate paddlers. As we dropped into the rapids, though, we realized we were in trouble because our skills were more in the beginner category.

Suddenly our canoe hit a rock and we turned broadside. The water rushed over our canoe. Tom and I were thrown into the rapids. As we tried to swim in the agitated water, we saw our canoe upside down on its way down the river. We floated downstream at a really fast pace. Finally, Tom and I were about 10 yards from each other, my brother behind me.

"Jim, catch my leg!" he yelled.

A few years earlier Tom had lost his leg in a hunting accident and had been fitted with a prosthetic one. He was wearing shorts and the leg had come off, rapidly floating downstream. Fortunately, just as the leg was whirling past me, I was able to reach out and grab it. It was full of water and extremely heavy, but I was able to get it to shore and then turn to help Tom, who was struggling. We were able to make it to safety. There happened to be a couple of people on the shore area who saw us and provided us with assistance. Tom and I were very grateful for their help.

As we were catching our breath, we saw our canoe about 30 yards away stuck between some rocks, but undamaged. Our fishing poles were gone, as well as everything, but we were able to retrieve our canoe with one paddle and continue downstream. About a mile further, we were very happy to see our cooler and recover it with our food and drink securely inside. We certainly couldn't fish anymore since our poles were lost in the rapids, but we could have lunch and enjoy the rest of the ride to Tom's truck. After the rapids, the waters were peaceful and we had time to think about how blessed we were to be alive. Tom also took the incident with much humor, laughing and telling me what a fisherman I was because I had been able to catch his leg floating down the rapids.

We came to our departure point, loaded up the canoe, and headed up the road back to my car. The most important thing, however, was that we lived to talk about it another day.

The Bees

In 1970 our family moved from 1209 West Hill Drive in Bedford, Virginia, to 1640 Oakwood Street, also in Bedford, Virginia. Our new home was on the corner lot and my wife and I had also purchased the lot next to us so we could have a large place for a garden, fruit and nut trees, and a small vineyard. We were the first home in North Hills in Bedford and we had a beautiful view of the Blue Ridge Mountains, only 11 miles away.

When I started to plant my many fruit and nut trees, garden, and vineyard, I decided that I needed to start raising honey bees. I liked honey and having the bees would be good for my trees, garden, and small vineyard. Within a short time, I acquired three beehives and placed them in our extra lot. I tried to read as much as possible about taking care of honey bees. I also had a great mentor. Joe Thaxton had been an industrial arts teacher at Bedford High School and his wife, Trudi, had been a biology teacher there. Both Joe and Trudi were wonderful mentors to me when I was a new teacher at Bedford High School. The couple was also very active at Main Street United Methodist Church where my family went. Now Joe, who had lots of experience with beekeeping, was retired and served as a teacher to me as I started beekeeping.

Unlike today, in the 1970s the honey bee population in Bedford was strong. Sadly, in the last decade the bee population has declined due to an invasive mite that not only feeds on the bees but also transmits viruses. In 1970, though, my hives were quickly thriving.

One late summer afternoon, the children came running in the house saying that the bees were flying all over the place. I walked down to the beehives and noticed on a small six-foot peach tree a large ball of bees. I recognized them as a swarm. A queen bee from one of the hives had left and taken many of the bees with her. I wanted to capture the swarm and add another hive. Unfortunately, I had a softball game and could not deal with it until after the game was over. The children were told not to go outside anywhere near it.

After the game I drove my truck down to the swarm and turned the headlights on the small tree. I knew that at dawn, the queen would leave and the bees in the swarm would follow. My plan was to take my extra hive that I had on hand and drop them into this new home. To protect me from bee stings, I put on my 1970s beekeeping suit which consisted of a hat and veil, special long pants and jacket, and long gloves. I then ventured out to move the swarm of bees into the new hive. As I began to work, I heard a male voice and saw two flashlights coming towards me. Two men identified themselves as police officers. I told them this was my property, my bees had swarmed, and I was trying to bring the bees into a new hive. Both of the city police officers instantly began to walk backwards cautiously away from the swarm. I returned to my work. I put the bees into their new home and placed this new hive next to the other three. I realized that I also needed to rob the hive from where the swarm came as soon as possible.

The next day was a very hot for late summer so I decided to wait to rob the hive until later in the day when it was cooler. That late afternoon, I put back on my beekeeping suit, got my smoker ready, and family and friends watched me at a distance in support. My plan was to remove the super that was sitting on the top of the hive, where the bees make the honey. That super was about two feet by three feet and included 10 frames that I was going to pull individually to remove the honey.

I took the top of the hive off and pumped the smoker. A smoker is used to calm the bees by masking the alarm pheromones that are released by guard bees or bees that are injured. After the smoke is pumped, this usually provides enough time for the beekeeper to work while the bees' defensive response is interrupted. My smoker was in excellent working order as a great deal of smoke came out. I removed the super and set it on the picnic table that was a short distance away. It was then that I began to feel stings on my legs and ankles.

I had made a mistake. I had on my white athletic socks and tennis shoes under my bee suit and I should have had on boots. I looked down and bees were all over me. I began to run towards the house to get away from them. The more I ran, the more stings I could feel. My wife saw me coming and got a broom and began knocking the bees off me. I finally got to the house and headed straight for the shower in the bedroom. As I turned on the water and took my clothes off, to my dismay I could still see more bees on me. By this time both of my ankles were beginning to burn and I was dizzy.

In a short time my ankles were swollen and I could not walk. I put on shorts and sat down in the chair in the den. My wife brought ice packs and we put them on both ankles. I didn't realize at the time that my life was in danger from being stung so many times. On my left leg and ankle I counted over 30 stings, and on the right I counted about 25.

That night I couldn't sleep and when I tried to walk, it was very painful. The next morning my wife drove me to the doctor's office. When I told Dr. Hardy what happened, he immediately gave me a shot and said, "Damn boy, you could have died from all these stings." Dr. Hardy explained further how serious it could have been if I had been allergic to bees. He reiterated that I could have died. He also made me stay in his office for a couple of hours, only allowing me to return home with a set of crutches. Later that day the swelling began to go down, but I still had trouble walking.

I have done some stupid things in my life, but this was the worst. I continued raising bees and my family enjoyed our honey for several years. And I never forgot again to cover up my ankles with more than just white athletic socks.

Wine Explosion

The Concord grape gets its name from Concord, Massachusetts, where it was developed. It is used for making jelly, juice, and wine. In 1854 Dr. Thomas Bramwell Welch invented grape juice using the Concord grape and the process of pasteurization that prevented the juice from fermenting. I had planted six Concord grape vines at our new home in Bedford in 1970. In a few years, the vines were covered with purple grapes and ready to be harvested. Justine made jelly and juice from the grapes. I made wine.

One August afternoon after football practice, I decided it was time to make some vino. I had read in the Bible that one of the first miracles Jesus did was to turn water into wine so I assured my wife that I could easily manage a homemade concoction.

My four children went to work picking the grapes while I gathered and sterilized my equipment. The plan was for me to wash the grapes in a giant tub and for my three sons, Mike, Ken, and Jeff, to take their shoes off and to stomp on the grapes squeezing out the juice. As a part of the crushing process, grape juice went to the top while grape skins rested on the bottom.

Justine and Cherie ensured that the boys' feet had been thoroughly cleaned. We let the boys stomp. They loved jumping up and down on the grapes and soon they were purple from their knees down. As they stomped and their legs became more purple, my wife and daughter watched from the shade laughing and saying, "We cannot believe this."

It was soon time to add yeast to the grape juice and put the juice in our gallon containers. We ended up with 10 gallons. I put on tops and stored five jars in the back bedroom and five in the basement. The last step was just to wait for the juice to ferment and turn to wine.

After about a week or so, at 2:00 in the morning, a very loud noise awakened the family. The noise came from the back bedroom where the five jars had been placed. Justine and I slowly opened the door to the bedroom and were shocked. It seemed like the whole room was purple. There was grape juice all over the walls, the curtains, the bed, and everything else in the room. It took hours for me to clean up the mess and after several days, Justine forgave me.

Yes, the jars had exploded because I had left the lids on them. Gas had built up in the jars causing them to explode. After researching the wine making process further, I learned later that I should have put a balloon on them to provide room for the gas to be released. Since the jars in the basement had not exploded, I put balloons on each of those jars. I then waited for the fermenting process to finish.

It was finally time to try out my wine. The substance *looked* like wine, but the taste was not sweet like my recipe had said it would be. It was more like vinegar and the batch had to be tossed. After further research, however, and more practice through the years, I eventually ended up with some good tasting homemade sweet wine.

Frog Gigging

In the state of Virginia, you can legally catch bullfrogs. They have big meaty legs and, if cooked right, they are a delicacy. Some say they taste better than chicken. I credit my mastery of frog gigging to the experiences on the banks of the Clinch River in Richlands. Several of my friends and I would go out at night on the banks of the Clinch gigging, basically like spearing fish. I would bring my catch of bullfrogs home and my mother would fry them up for us to eat for dinner.

As a young father, during the summer months, I took my four young children with me to gig frogs in Bedford County. There were several ponds nearby and when it got dark, we started our adventure.

Each of the kids was given a flashlight and I carried the two gigging poles, attaching sharp tines to the end of each. The kids and I headed to our favorite pond and listened for the deep croaking of the bullfrogs. We cautiously tiptoed to where we heard loud croaking to shine a light looking for their reflective eyes. We found huge bullfrogs that matched their loud croaks. Some had legs three and four inches long. My three sons caught on quickly and learned how to be good giggers. (Most importantly, they never gigged themselves or one another.) While my daughter went gigging with us, she did not enjoy the actual spearing but still helped look for bullfrogs.

I will never forget the first time I took my four children gigging. We brought back about 15 large ones. We had put the gigged frogs in a potato sack and tied the top of the bag. We took the frogs home that night and dumped them into the kitchen sink to clean. The next thing we knew, four of the frogs jumped out of the sink and onto the kitchen floor. We had a time catching them! Justine was not happy with bloody bullfrogs jumping on her clean floor. I learned really fast to make sure the bullfrogs were dead before we brought them home. After I cleaned them by cutting their legs off and peeling their skin back, I gave the legs to my wife and said to cook them like chicken. She did very well, although cooking frog legs took some getting used to because, as you might know, they sometimes jump in the frying pan when cooked. As our gigging adventures continued, the special recipe Justine used made them taste even better than chicken.

The most memorable gigging adventure was right after I purchased a canoe made of leather. One summer night we went back to our favorite pond and launched it into the water. Without warning, a big bullfrog jumped in with us. My youngest son quickly tried to gig it but instead of spearing the frog his pole missed and poked holes through the bottom of the leather. We soon began to take on water. The kids were bailing us out until I could to get the boat to shore. Fortunately, we made it before the canoe completely sank.

That was one lucky bullfrog.

Fire Drill at Myrtle Beach

Nearly every summer I taught summer school so we could have the money to go on a nice vacation the first week in August right before football season started. Our favorite vacation spot was Myrtle Beach. In 1974, my mother had purchased a Class C motorhome with the plan of allowing her three children to take it out camping with their families. It was then that we started vacationing with the camper, which cost us a lot less money than staying in a motel.

We loved the beach and parked our camper very close to the Atlantic Ocean where we heard waves breaking on the beach. Our children spent all morning at the beach, came in for lunch, went to the swimming pool late in the afternoon, and visited arcades at night. Justine fixed a delicious meal each evening on the gas stove.

On one of our first days, the children were worn out due to the excitement of the beach. They were taking a late afternoon nap and my wife was cooking super in the camper. I rode my bicycle to the camp store to pick up some supplies for dinner.

As I was returning I cruised down my street and saw a huge cloud of smoke from our camper. As I got closer, I watched my whole family running out saying it was on fire. I went into the motorhome, found the fire extinguisher, and began looking for the fire, but found nothing to spray. There was no fire.

My family was lined up a good distance away like they were practicing a fire drill. All the neighbors were standing around watching us.

As I was exiting the motorhome to check its exterior, I saw a truck spraying chemicals. Mosquitoes were really bad in the park and every night about 6:00, they sent the truck out to spray the entire campground. For some reason the truck had stopped at our campsite and continued to release its cloud of chemicals. This was the smoke I had seen surrounding our entire motorhome. The smoke was so strong that it had seeped into our camper. This was when my four children woke up and ran out of the camper with my wife.

Everyone began laughing when we realized what had happened and I was relieved that I did not have to use my fire extinguisher. We took the kids to McDonald's that night and knew from then on to prepare for the mosquito spray around 6:00 each evening.

Now, I think about those chemicals the park sprayed every evening and how they might have affected the health of the campers. We had no mosquitoes, but what toll did the chemicals take on everyone?

South of the Border

Crossing the border in 1975 from San Diego to Tijuana was not like it is in the 21st century. For example, when traveling from San Diego to Tijuana and back for someone from Virginia, no passport was needed. There was still, however, extensive searching of vehicles done by the border patrol, especially when coming from Mexico into San Diego. Tijuana in 1975 was also much different than it is today. In 1975, the population of Tijuana was only 355,000 whereas today the population is 2,181,000.

We had been visiting my cousin, Linda Glass, in Bakersfield, California, and our plan was to travel into Tijuana to visit and to shop. My cousin had given us some pointers about purchasing Mexico insurance in case we "were ripped off" and had told us never to accept the price of what we were first told, but to negotiate, or bargain. With my insurance and bargaining skills rehearsed, we set out on our journey across the border.

As we traveled south from Bakersfield we passed Los Angeles. Approaching L.A. we noticed a large cloud of smoke that hung over the city. Smog. Pollution over L.A. was substantial. Of all the cities I have visited, I have never seen such smog that hung over a city as this. I was more than pleased not to be stopping there.

We soon arrived in San Diego and prepared to cross the border into Mexico. The border patrol officers from Mexico were very nice. They politely asked me a lot of questions and looked all through our motorhome, being very respectful to our children. After about one hour, including waiting in line, we were approved and able to cross into Mexico.

Driving into the streets of Tijuana, the family could immediately tell they were in another country. The city was dirty and the standard of living at a much lower level. It was shocking to see such a difference from just a few miles down the road. I soon found a lot to park the motorhome so the family could begin exploring the city. As soon as I cut the engine off, there were as many as 30 young boys who surrounded our vehicle and started saying repeatedly in broken English, "Watch car!" I finally figured out that these boys were offering to watch our motorhome for us while we visited. I got out of the motorhome and picked out five boys. I told them they could watch our motorhome while we were gone. I gave them each $1.00 and said I would give them another dollar when we returned.

The shops we visited were full of souvenir type gifts as well as different types of clothing. Justine and Cherie found some handmade suede jackets, navy blue for Cherie and tan for Justine, and I purchased them. The jackets were of very good quality and at less than half the cost of what they would have been in the United States. Justine also found the boys some cloth jackets that I bought for them. All the jackets turned out to be very durable. In fact, Cherie and Justine wore their jackets for many years to come. We also got some souvenir type items such as a glow-in-the-dark Snoopy picture that hangs in my house today and has been spoken for by my granddaughter, Alison. We ended up spending less than $100.00 for some very nice items.

When we returned to the parking lot, we saw the five boys I had hired standing around our motorhome, and the other crowd of boys also standing in the lot. After my family entered the motorhome, I took the five boys I had hired aside and gave them each $2.00, but I gave the money to them privately so the other boys would not see them get it. They seemed very happy to have earned $3.00 for just a few hours.

We were soon on our way back into the United States but as we approached the border, we saw six lanes of traffic at a standstill. We knew getting back into the United States was going to take a lot longer. Finally, it was our turn to talk to the border patrol. They first interviewed me asking if I had a weapon or more than $5,000 in cash. After answering their questions, "No, I did not have a weapon" and "No, I did not have more than $5,000 in cash," they asked me why I was in Tijuana. I explained that I had taken my wife and children across the border to see the city and do some shopping. They boarded my motorhome. Once inside they opened all compartments, even the refrigerator and little freezer. The officers were especially polite and kind to the four children and even joked with them a little bit.

I was asked to come outside the motorhome with my keys and they told me to open the outdoor compartments to search those areas as well. After we were given permission to proceed, we saw a group of drug dogs with their handlers. We also passed by several vans whose occupants were standing outside their vehicles in handcuffs. After seeing the scene of dogs, officers, and people in handcuffs, I was not surprised why the traffic had been at a standstill and was so backed up.

Back in the United States, we proceeded to San Diego and camped at Mission Bay. We had a wonderful time camping right on the bay and fishing. The next day we went to the San Diego Zoo, which was the best zoo I had ever visited.

As our return journey took us past Los Angeles, we again saw the cloud of smog and rolled up our windows. Coming from the foot of the Peaks of Otter in Bedford, our noses were definitely not used to the dry stench that came with the smog. With windows up, we turned on our small TV that drew its electricity from the cigarette lighter and was able to pick up the local station through its antenna. As interesting as Los Angeles might have been, with the rolled-up windows the children preferred the TV programs.

Flying Down the Snake River

In June of 1975 we loaded up our four young children in a Class C motorhome and took off for California. After touring the western United States and Mexico, we started back to Virginia. The return trip would take us over the Sierra Nevada Mountains into Nevada and down to Jackson Hole, Wyoming. It was there that we planned to rest and have some more fun.

One item on my bucket list was to take the family on a "float" trip down the Snake River in Wyoming. In addition to scenic floating trips on flat water, or what is classified as Class I whitewater rafting, the Snake River is also known to have the best whitewater in the United States. In June and July, the Snake River is fed by the runoff of snow in the mountains and is very fast and high. The water is icy cold with water temperatures as low as the mid-40s. Whitewater river classifications range from I to V. In the early summer, the Snake River whitewater can get up as high as Class IV.

On a cold and cloudy afternoon, I purchased our tickets for $125.00. The fee included a river guide who ensured we would get safely down the eight miles of water. The man who sold me the tickets told me to be at the river the next morning at 9:00 a.m. and also mentioned something about not eating a big breakfast.

The next morning it was raining but we arrived right on time and saw our "float," actually a rubber raft about 10 x 8 feet, big enough for our family of six plus six more. We were to be the second of three rafts launching just south of Jackson Hole. We suited up in life jackets, boarded the raft, and met our guide. Before we launched, he talked to us for 15 minutes about safety and what to expect. We noticed how he looked like a linebacker with enormous muscles and kept a very intense look on his face. The kids whispered that he resembled Kojak because of his shaven head. After telling us he would navigate from the center of the raft with long paddles, he explained what we were to do when we came to the rapids. He showed us a rope around the inside of the raft and said, "When we hit the whitewater, you will need to get down on all fours and hang on to the rope. Do not try to stand up!" Justine looked over at me with horror. She was expecting to take the scenic "float" trip; I had not mentioned to her anything about rapids.

"The raft," continued the guide, "will hit the rapids hard and white-water will force us up in the air." After some discussion about how high we would be forced upward, he concluded, "You are all going to get wet," and we launched. It was now too late for any member of the family to get off the raft. All we could do was to hang on tight.

As we started down the river, I pulled out my large 1975 video camera that I had covered in plastic wrap under my coat. The guide frowned at me when he saw it. "I brought my movie camera with me because I want to video this trip of a lifetime," I said to him.

The guide told me: "Your camera is going to get wet and it will not work. It will be ruined."

I decided to accept the risk.

We soon saw that the river was running fast and learned it was actually running faster than usual. In about a half mile, the river narrowed and the rapids roared so loud we could no longer hear anyone talk. As we hunkered down on all fours and held tight to the rope, our guide used his muscles and paddled as hard as he could. The whitewater then hit the raft hard and the front propelled upward with water gushing over us as we came down, so hard we felt like we were directly under a waterfall. I looked over at my three sons who were laughing, my daughter who was not, and my wife who was wet with the cold water. We came to calm water and were able to sit up in our raft, loosen our grips from the rope, and hear each other talk. I believe my daughter and wife were talking about the scenic route. I told them I had gotten some great pictures. In these first calming waters, we could see that the lead raft made it through safely, but we could not see the raft behind us anywhere. In fact, we never saw the raft behind us again.

We took many more sets of rapids with calming waters in between. We found the last set the most intimidating as we watched the lead raft about 50 yards in front of us quickly disappear. We heard it was the biggest section of all. We made it through with no problems, and I continued to get some wonderful pictures.

In total we had traveled about eight miles and ran what I thought was about seven or eight rapids, but it could have been more. With each set, we grew to appreciate our guide's strength and skill to keep us afloat in this unusually fast water.

When we came to the end of our run, we were given blankets, hot chocolate, and taken in a van back to our departure point. It was confirmed that the reason we never saw the raft behind us was because it had capsized in the first set of rapids and the people had to be rescued by employees on the bank that the rafting company had stationed.

The next day we loaded up our motorhome and headed south to Yellowstone National Park, ready for another adventure and the opportunity to use my video camera. Today, the kids still talk about the trip and I am grateful that Justine forgave me, even if it took a few days.

Yellowstone Adventures

Our family had been on the road for about three weeks when we entered the North Entrance of Yellowstone National Park in Wyoming. We were traveling in a Class C motorhome. Our trip had started from our home in Bedford, Virginia. We crossed the Mississippi River at Memphis, Tennessee, and went as far west as Bakersfield, California, where one of my first cousins lived. We spent a week in California, visited Mexico, and we were heading back to Virginia visiting national parks along the way. After riding in the motorhome for so long, the children needed some hands-on activities and Yellowstone was a welcoming sight.

Soon after entering the park, we started to see wildlife such as grizzly bears, elk, and bison. Since prehistoric times, bison have freely roamed the Yellowstone area. Sadly, bison almost became extinct as they were hunted during the 1800s. By 1902 poachers had killed off so many of the bison that there were only about two dozen left. At the beginning of the 20th century, the U.S. Army, who was in charge of the park, protected the bison from further poaching. Today, the bison herd number is over 5,000.

Our plan was to spend two days in the park, but we were overwhelmed by the many unique sights and realized we needed much more time. After we crossed into the Yellowstone National Park, we passed the Mammoth Hot Springs, Obsidian Cliff, and visited the Old Faithful geyser. Every hour Old Faithful erupted by spewing hot water into the air. The geysers, hot springs, and mud pots generated many questions from the children, ages 13 (Cherie), 10 (Kenneth), 10 (Michael), and 9 (Jeffrey). After we watched Old Faithful erupt, we walked for about 15 or more minutes to the Black Sand Basin area to see another geyser. As we were watching it, we experienced a special grand finale that caught us off guard. We first heard a sound like a train coming through and then the ground under our feet rocked back and forth and we were knocked down to the ground from a standing position. We were in the midst of an earthquake. Justine collected the children and tried to get them away from the geyser, but it was slow going with the ground shaking so violently. I could not tell where she was taking the children, but this was one time that she outran me. I do not think she knew where she was going except to get away from the geyser. Finally, we were all at a safer distance and we stopped to hunker down until the quake passed.

The next day, we traveled east to Fishing Bridge, Wyoming, which was on the north of Yellowstone Lake. Yellowstone Lake is the largest natural high elevation lake in North America at 20 miles long and 14 miles wide. We parked the motorhome at Fishing Bridge and walked to the marina. The three boys wanted to fish in the lake. I purchased a license for me and rented a small boat at the marina. The park rangers told us to be careful because the water temperature in the lake was 40 degrees. They also reminded us to be sure to wear our life preservers. In Virginia, we fished for rainbow and brown trout, but at Yellowstone Lake we were preparing to fish for its native cutthroat trout. The boys and I were excited because we were told we could each keep three of the cutthroats. I loaded the boys and their fishing poles in the boat and we headed out into Yellowstone Lake.

Soon after leaving the marina, my youngest Jeff saw a "black cow" on the bank. We drifted towards this but when it raised its head from eating the tall grass next to the lake, we saw that the "black cow" was actually a 1000-pound moose with a six-foot rack. Fortunately, it ignored us and continued to eat as we floated away.

After fishing in the lake for over an hour, we had only caught a few fish. We headed back to the marina to meet Justine and Cherie. On the way, however, we started catching more fish just within 20 minutes. The three boys each had caught two. It was then that I heard a voice over the loudspeaker calling for boat 217, which was us, to return to shore. As soon as we landed, we were greeted by two park rangers. They told me we were breaking the law by fishing in the marina and they would have to give me a ticket. My wife, however, came to my rescue when she defended me by telling the park rangers that this was unfair because the sign that said "no fishing" was not visible due to being covered with brush. After talking for 10 minutes about the unfairness of the ticket, the park rangers agreed not to give me a ticket if we threw our fish back in the lake and they lived. We threw all the fish back and watched them swim off. The boys were tearing up because they couldn't have them for supper and did not understand. I made it up to them with ice cream at the camp store, and soon everything was okay.

The next morning, we headed out of the Yellowstone Park toward the East Entrance and Sylvan Pass. In the distance as we left, we saw Eagle Peak, which is the highest point in the park at 11,372 feet. We were further inspired by the landscape as we traveled toward home.

That night, I explained to the children that Yellowstone was founded in 1872. I told them that before Americans came to Yellowstone, several Native American Indian tribes, such as the Crow, Shoshone, Blackfeet, and Nez Perce, had lived in the area. I explained that over the years several Indian wars were fought over the land and how the U.S. Cavalry came in during the 1880s to protect American tourists. As the U.S. Cavalry protected the tourists, they discouraged the Native Americans from even hunting on the 2.2 million acres of land. We discussed how the U.S. government did not treat the Native Americans fairly and how the U.S. acquired an amazing national park but "at what cost."

Rabbit Hunting

Ever since my brother's hunting accident in 1960, I had not been overly enthusiastic about hunting. Nevertheless, I knew how important it was for my sons to have the experience and to learn how to do so safely.

When my three sons were big enough to hunt, I bought each boy a single barrel shotgun. It could only hold one shell and had to be broken down and reloaded. I spent a lot of time talking to them about gun safety and took all three hunting several times. One fall, however, my sons and I were invited to go rabbit hunting with some of my friends. One of the men had about 15 beagles that were trained to chase rabbits. Hunting with dogs would be a totally new experience for my sons.

One morning we met at a location in Bedford County. The owner of the beagles opened the dogs' cages and let them go. We never heard so much barking in our lives. The dogs were more than ready to chase rabbits. My friends we were hunting with talked about how the night before it had been a full moon. They said the bright moonlight was especially good because it encouraged the rabbits to go out during the night and stay in their burrows during the day and sleep. As a result, it would be much easier for the dogs to chase the rabbits out of their burrows.

I really appreciated how the owner of the beagles gave instructions to my sons about how to hunt with dogs. He told them that after the dogs found the rabbits, they would be placed about 30 yards from each other, yet at a location where they could see the chase as best as possible. Most importantly he told my sons that they were not to move and to stay put after they were placed in their location. He described to them how the dogs would chase the rabbits and to let the animals do the work. After some other words of instructions, the dogs were released and jumped the rabbits. My three sons were placed in safe locations 30 yards apart from each other.

The boys watched in amazement as the 15 dogs worked driving the rabbits back to them. The boys were then told when they could shoot. They shot and shot and finally each one had killed a rabbit. The men in the group each took a turn getting into safe positions and waiting for the dogs to drive the rabbits back to them. The group of men shot about 15 rabbits but asked my sons how many they would like to take home. My boys said five. I had to intervene and say only two because I knew I would be cleaning the rabbits, and that cooking them would be a new experience for Justine who was still getting over her frog legs experience.

When we returned home to Bedford, my wife met us at the door and pointed us in the direction of the basement. The boys and I cleaned the two rabbits. The next night, Justine fixed a delicious rabbit stew for supper.

My sons and I continued to hunt in the years to come, shooting crows and doves. We were also invited to hunt on my brother Tom's property in Elon, Virginia. There, each of my sons killed a deer. While these hunting experiences were an important part of their growing up, nothing compared to the day they had the opportunity to hunt with the dogs and watch the chase.

Wolf Moon

Sharp Top Mountain, one of the two peaks that make up the Peaks of Otter, is located next to the Blue Ridge Parkway, about eight miles from Bedford, Virginia. It rises 3,862 feet high and is paired with its twin peak, Flat Top, which rises 4,001 feet high. Through the years, Sharp Top has captivated a lot of people. Thomas Jefferson was so impressed with its size that he thought it was the tallest mountain in the United States and in 1815 used chains and trigonometry to estimate the height of the mountain. In the mid-19th century, Bedford citizens thought Sharp Top was the "loftiest" mountain in Virginia. Around 1852-1853, the citizens of Bedford took one of the granite rocks from Sharp Top, also known as Otter's Summit, and sent it to be displayed in the Washington Monument. The inscription on the rock reads, "FROM OTTER'S SUMMIT, VIRGINIA'S LOFTIEST PEAK. TO CROWN A MONUMENT TO VIRGINIA'S NOBLEST SON."

But what I really want to tell you about is something that has been known only to the old lofty mountain and four young men. It was about 45 years ago that four Bedford County public school educators flew off the mountain. It was a cold January Sunday night around 1976. School had been canceled on Monday because of the snow and cold. The plan was to drive up to Sharp Top from Bedford, take our sleds with us, hike all the way to the summit, and then sleigh ride down the 10-foot-wide road that was used to transport sightseers by small bus.

It took us over two and a half hours to make the trip up the mountain carrying our sleds. There was a Wolf Moon and standing on the summit we could see for miles, 360 degrees in every direction. The Shenandoah Valley was to the north, Lynchburg to the east, Smith Mountain Lake to the south, and Roanoke to the west. As we came off the summit and to the top of the road, we noticed it was like an ice rink. That week it had snowed about eight inches, melting and refreezing.

Nevertheless, the plan was still for Jim Grobe to go first. Jim was the football coach at Liberty High School and would later become the head coach at Wake Forest University, where he would earn the title of National Coach of the Year, then become the head coach at Baylor University. Marion Hargrove would go second. He had been a principal in Bedford County and would later become the assistant superintendent for Bedford County Public Schools. Denzil Barker was also a principal in Bedford County and would become the Director of Personnel for Bedford County Public Schools. At this time, I was a teacher and head baseball coach at Liberty High, the coordinator of this event, and the plan was for me to go last.

We knew we would be going fast, but we did not know until later just *how* fast. We finally took off with about 15 seconds between each man. Just as planned, Grobe was first, Hargrove second, Barker third, and myself last. I hadn't gone 50 yards when I ran into Denzil who had crashed on the first steep curve. When I hit him, he knocked me off the road and into a boulder. By the time I got back on the road, Denzil was already recovered and on his way down the mountain. I could not see the others, but I could hear them in the distance howling as they flew off the mountain under the bright moon. I was going so quick that my eyes watered and my vision blurred. I could, however, smell the leather and rubber from the boots of the three who had gone ahead of me. They had made serious efforts trying to dig their feet into the ice attempting to slow down. While it took over two and a half hours to hike to the top, it only took 15 minutes to sleigh ride off the mountain.

We four made it home that January night, thankful we were able to return to our families and jobs as God was watching over us. Three of us are now already in our eighties and we are fortunate to still be able to get together and reminisce about the night, 45 years ago, that we flew off Sharp Top Mountain under the Wolf Moon.

The Miracle Season

It was 1977, and I had been coaching varsity baseball for 17 years, four years at Bedford High School and 13 years at Liberty High School in Bedford, Virginia. This year we had an exceptional season, winning the regular Seminole District with a record of 17 wins and only three losses. Even with such an outstanding season, we lost the district tournament to Jefferson Forest High School, another Bedford County School just 13 miles away. Their coach, Kelly Russell, had been one of my former high school baseball players, so the loss was bittersweet. Fortunately, winning the regular season, we were still invited to compete in the regional tournament.

That year the regional tournament was to be held in Covington, Virginia, and our first opponent was a team from the farthest area away, Patrick County. Harold Jones, my assistant coach, and I loaded our Liberty Minutemen on the old yellow school bus and we traveled over the Allegheny Mountains for an afternoon game.

To win at baseball, you must have talent, skill, heart, and strategy. We had a very talented team that had practiced hard mastering the fundamentals of baseball, and they had clearly shown me during the regular season that they had heart. Now they needed strategy from their coaches. In a tournament where numerous games are played, if the team continues to be successful and win, one of the most important pieces of strategy for a coach is knowing which pitcher to use and when. Harold Jones and I made the decision to pitch Lamie Haga that first game, and it was a wise choice. Lamie pitched an outstanding game and we scored some runs, winning 6 to 2.

In the meantime, Jefferson Forest had lost a tight game and was eliminated from the region. In high school baseball, if you lost one game in the tournament, you were out. It was a tough requirement.

Our next game was against the Blue Ridge district champions, Allegheny High School. We were scheduled to play at 10:00 on a Saturday morning. We loaded old yellow very early in the morning and traveled 76 miles. When we arrived at the stadium on this very hot morning, there were several thousand fans already in the stands.

For this regional game, Harold Jones (who was the pitching coach and called the pitches) and I thought hard again about which pitcher to use. After studying the strengths of our opponent and considering our own strengths, we made the decision to start our number one pitcher, Donald Minnick. He was left-handed and could throw the ball over 90 miles per hour. Donald had only lost one game during the regular season. He pitched a strong game and we won 6 to 1. We hit the ball well, and our Liberty Minutemen also made some impressive plays in the field to help Donald out.

The win against Allegheny High School propelled us into the final game of the regionals, which was to begin that same night at 7:00. This time we would be playing the champions from the Piedmont District, Drewry Mason High School.

We started the game with another left-handed pitcher, Ron Jones. He pitched a very good game and in the sixth inning we brought in Donald Minnick to close. Donald gave us two strong innings while the rest of the team continued to play exceptional defense. We earned the title of Region III Champions. After the ceremony, we loaded up again on the hot old yellow school bus and rode 76 miles back to Bedford, Virginia. Our young men were real troupers.

In Virginia, there were four regions, two in the western part of the state and two in the eastern part. We were in the western section. Representing Region III, we were now considered to be one of the four best teams in Virginia. On Sunday, we learned we would be playing Virginia High School, the Region II Champions. Their record was 20 wins and only one loss. One part of our scouting report told Coach Jones and me that this team had a large number of exceptional players, so we knew this team was going to be tough competition. Our game was scheduled for Tuesday evening at 7:00 in Bristol, Virginia.

I had requested a charter bus to take our team to this state semifinal game, but was told there was no money for it. I was able, however, to obtain funding for the team to stay in a motel so we would not be getting home at 3:00 in the morning. I definitely did not like the thought of our young men riding a school bus on Interstate 81 in the early hours, so I was grateful that I was at least able to get the overnight trip approved on such short notice and to secure the funding for the motel.

On Tuesday morning, we loaded up on our old yellow school bus *again* and headed west for Bristol, which was about 140 miles south on Interstate 81. After riding on the school bus for three and a half hours, we arrived at our motel and had the opportunity to rest a little.

It was soon time to go to the game. We were playing in a minor league stadium that had a large capacity for seating. When we arrived at the ballpark, there were already thousands of fans in the stands. It was a little intimidating to see so many people, even more so since the fans were not nice to us when our team walked by them in the stands.

We settled in on our side of the field. It was cloudy that night and damp, not exceptional conditions for a state semifinal game. Coach Jones and I discussed our pitching strategy again and made the final decision to start Donald Minnick on the mound. We told Donald not to overthrow. His fastball was in the low 90s and we knew it was going to be hard to get him to save the pitches.

During the first inning, Ron Jones helped get the momentum going by hitting a two-run homer. Donald Minnick was bringing the heat. In the first three innings he struck out eight; he ended up with 17 strikeouts and gave up only four hits. Again, the team made the plays defensively and we were off to the state championship game.

Afterward, Coach Harold Jones came to me and said he had just talked to his wife by phone and she informed him that she was in labor. My wife had driven to Bristol with all four of our children. I made arrangements for Justine and our kids to ride the bus back with the team and me. Harold then took my wife's car and left for Bedford at 11:00 p.m. His trip home went well except for his being stopped by a state police officer because he was going 87 mph down Interstate 81. After explaining that his wife was in labor and that he was trying to get back to Bedford before the baby was born, the trooper had mercy on him and let him off with a warning. After Harold returned to Bedford, it was determined his wife had false labor pains.

In the meantime, the team and I had returned to the hotel. Before I turned in for the night, I made my final rounds checking on the guys in their rooms. In one of them, I found five of my starters with something that was against the team rules, a certain beverage. I said nothing to the boys. I just looked at them with disappointment and then walked out of their room because I was furious. They knew they were in serious trouble with me. I will never forget the expression on their faces when I walked in their room. I never knew exactly who brought them their little beverage from Bedford, but I later heard that a couple of students, who had come to the game, had dropped it off as a present, trying to be cute. My five ball players lost their minds momentarily and forgot their focus. They knew I would be helping them remember their focus in the days ahead.

The next morning, we left Bristol for home with some sad faces. No one said a word on the ride back that was over three hours. When we got back to Bedford, I made arrangements to meet with the five boys and Coach Jones in the coaches' office as soon as possible. Coach Jones and I told the boys how disappointed we were with them. They were then told to see me in my classroom at 7:30 the next morning to discuss the matter further.

After praying about the situation, I decided to run the boys on the track at Liberty High School for two hours before and after their regularly scheduled practices. I would also have them write a letter of apology and then I would think further about letting them play on Friday. The boys wrote their letters and ran hard before and after their practices.

It was soon Friday, game day. We were scheduled to play Randolph Henry High School for the state championship. This would make our fifth game played in less than a week.

School was closed on Friday so the students of Liberty could come to the game. The game was to be played at City Stadium in Lynchburg. Watts Key, the WBLT disc jockey, would broadcast the game to Bedford County so those who didn't come could tune in and listen. Several church groups made preparations to use their buses to bring students to the game. All the local TV stations were there as well as the *Lynchburg News, Roanoke Times* and of course the *Bedford Bulletin.* Justine and our children were all in attendance. My sons Ken, Mike, and Jeff served as bat boys. My wife was charged with taking a video of the game. Harold's wife, Margie, was there to cheer us on even though she was expecting her baby at any moment.

No one spoke a word during the 23-mile trip on our old yellow school bus to City Stadium in Lynchburg on that Friday. The five still did not know my final decision as to whether they would play or not. I was still thinking and praying about it.

It was not until we filed into City Stadium and began our pregame drills that my decision was finally made. I walked over to Donald Minnick and handed him the game ball. He knew he was pitching and the other four were starting the game.

This was going to be a game for the ages.

We were the home team. Donald Minnick struck out the side the first inning on only nine pitches, all strikes. In the bottom of the first inning, Donnie McKinney laid down a great bunt for Jim Thacker to score on a squeeze play. We were up one to nothing. Our defense was solid, but Randolph Henry scored one run in the fourth and another in the fifth inning, which gave them the lead at two to one. We told Lamie Haga to start throwing in the bullpen.

Donald was getting tired, and in the sixth (next to last) inning, I went to the mound to talk to him. His shirt was out, his hat was crooked, and he was sweating. I told him Haga was ready to come in. Randolph Henry had a runner on second base with two outs. I asked him, "Donald, can you get one more out, and we will bring in Lamie in the last inning?" He said he could, and the next batter grounded out to Phillip Nichols at second base to end the inning. We went to the bottom of the sixth inning down two to one.

In that inning, Jim Thacker and Ron Jones got on base with two outs. Donald came to bat. The coach from Patrick Henry brought the left fielder in because his scouting report said that Minnick could not hit. On the first pitch, Minnick hit the ball over the left fielder's head all the way to the fence. Both Thacker and Jones scored. Minnick was thrown out at third base after I had tried to stop him at second. He later told me he had wanted to get to the dugout and rest.

With a three to two lead going into the last inning, I looked in the dugout and Lamie was ready to go into the game. Minnick said, "Coach, let me try, and if I get in trouble, bring in Lamie." So, I kept him in as pitcher. Donald walked the lead-off batter. He struck out the next batter, and the next one grounded out. The base runner stole second base with two outs, and made a break for third base. Our catcher, Tim Murphy, ran right at the base runner and forced him back to second base. I went to the mound and called in the whole infield and told them, "Don't worry about the runner on second. Donald, we have come a long way, and you have one more batter, then Haga can come in if needed."

Donald replied, "Give me the ball, Coach, and let's go."

The runner on second would go about halfway to third base, and Murphy would run him back. I told Coach Jones to throw this batter nothing but fast balls. The count was two balls and two strikes when Minnick threw a 93 miles per hour fastball. And struck the batter out! We were the state champions! The team had played five games in less than a week and traveled over 550 miles on old yellow to bring home the first state championship in Liberty High School's history.

That evening, when I got home, I was looking forward to watching the video of the game that Justine had filmed on our big old, bulky video recorder. However, she informed me that she wasn't able to film the game, because at first, she was too nervous and shaky to hold the camera steady. She also told me that she didn't even look at the game the last two innings because she had her head down and was praying. Although I was disappointed not to have the video to see, I think her praying was more important!

The day after the State Championship, June 4th, Margie went into labor early in the morning and Harold took her to the hospital. This time she was not having false labor pains and an hour after arriving at the hospital, Shawn Marie was born to Harold and Margie Jones. Margie recalls that the only thing the doctor wanted to talk about to Harold was Liberty winning the state baseball championship the day before. It was an exciting time for our families, all the players, their families, the school, and especially the Bedford community.

Incident at Liberty High School

I was beginning my twenty-first year of teaching and coaching at Liberty. The public school had an enrollment of just over 1000 students and was considered to be rural with several small communities in the county feeding into it, along with the Town of Bedford. The student body worked hard academically and excelled athletically. There was a lot of school pride among the students and the staff.

One day, however, things were not okay. In my building, I heard a loud gunshot that had come from the other side of the building. As I moved in the direction of the blast, I saw through the windows into the courtyard a young lady running down the hallway headed toward the main office. As I watched in horror, I also noticed a rather large young male with a shotgun following her down the hall. This was the gun that I had heard go off. I made sure students were locked in their classrooms.

Just moments earlier, the young man had entered a class near the parking lot where the young lady, his girlfriend, was sitting. The young man had pointed the shotgun around the room at the teacher and the students. The situation escalated and the young man fired his gun at the ceiling blowing a large hole in the roof. As the young man was reloading his 12-gauge, the young lady took off running out of the classroom to the office.

The teacher in the room next to where the shot was fired was my wife, Justine. Upon hearing the shot, she had gone to her door and locked it immediately. She then had the window shades pulled down and ordered the students to huddle together away from the door and the windows. The young lady made it to the main office and hid in a back room. But the shooter still followed her into the office with his gun. Staff who worked in the main office had already heard of the imminent danger and hid behind their desks. Some staff, such as Mrs. JoAnn Hancock, quickly moved a student into an area closet and then climbed in for protection.

Not finding the young lady in the office, the shooter opened a side door to leave the building. As he opened the door and before he stepped outside the building, Sheriff Carl Wells came from behind the shooter and safely grabbed him in a bear hug. The sheriff had been in the office and was waiting for the right moment to apprehend the male. Within seconds, deputies rushed to help the sheriff put the shooter in custody.

The reason the sheriff and deputies were already on the scene was because a teacher who had been in the parking lot had seen the shooter with the gun. Immediately this teacher got to a phone and called the main office, which then called the police. While the shooter was in the classroom with the teacher and the students, the sheriff and deputies were already en route and had actually arrived on campus before the shooter had made his way into the main office.

There were many heroes this day at Liberty High School. One hero was the teacher who had seen the young male in the parking lot with the shotgun and had the quick thinking to immediately call for help. The response of the Bedford County Sheriff's Office was more than outstanding as they were on the scene in minutes, and the main hero of the day was Sheriff Carl Wells, who took the shooter into custody safely from behind. Thankfully, no one was hurt that day.

A few months later, I was standing outside the main office with three other coaches. We heard a verbal altercation and I turned to see what was happening. It was the young man who had served his consequences and was back on campus. He was upset with the school administration. An administrator was yelling and the young man started to charge at the administrator. The coaches intervened and restrained the young man. One coach's glasses were broken and his face was bruised from the incident. I tried to talk to the young man and help him. It was a very unfortunate situation.

Months later, my doorbell rang and this young man was at my door wanting to talk to me. When you are a teacher, you care for your students as if they were your own children. This young man had already endured his consequences from the school and law enforcement. I would not turn the young man away and so I invited him into the house. We sat down and talked in my living room. He said he had come to say how sorry he was about everything that had happened. If this young man was going to have a future, I knew he needed to feel hope and encouragement. This was one of the most important teachable moments in my career, and I tried to get it right because I wanted him to be able to move forward with his life.

This young man grew up to be a good citizen in our community and a fine father. He worked to encourage other fathers and sons to do things together like play basketball on Sunday afternoons.

I never forgot this young man and how he came to my home to talk and to apologize. I hope in some small way I helped make a positive difference in his life.

The Olympic Festival

In the spring of 1986, after I had been coaching for 26 years, I received a letter in the mail that was from the U.S. Olympic Committee. It informed me that I had been selected to serve as one of three coaches for the East Baseball Team at the Olympic Festival to be held in Houston during the month of July. Accepting the invitation would mean I would travel to Houston and participate as a coach in the festival for 10 days. All of the games would be held at Rice University along with many of the practices. Other practices would be held at the Astrodome, which had a seating capacity of about 60,000 and was air conditioned.

Since 1978 the U.S. Olympic Committee has been holding these festivals, originally known as the National Sports Festival, during the years between the Olympic Games. They give athletes the opportunity to develop their skills and prepare for the Olympics. I had no idea I was being considered for the honor of coaching baseball for the East Olympic Baseball Team. The fact that the committee had sought me out was a tremendous honor. I immediately accepted the invitation and never regretted my decision, for the opportunity turned out to be a highlight in my baseball coaching career.

In July of that year, I left Bedford and traveled to Roanoke where I caught my flight to Charlotte and from there to Houston. This was a unique experience for me because I was going from a very rural area nestled in the mountains of Virginia to one of the largest metropolitan areas in the United States. In addition, even though I had been to nearly every state in our country, I had traveled by motorhome and had never flown anywhere. The attendant on the flight to Houston took good care of me. She made sure I had a seat next to the window so I could finally get that 30,000-foot view I had heard so much about. She also checked on me from time to time and came by when we passed over points of interest, such as the Mississippi River, making sure I did not miss it. After a while, the captain came on the intercom and said, "We are now on an approach to Houston Intercontinental Airport. We are 90 miles away, but we will be there in 20 minutes." I thought to myself, this plane is moving pretty fast.

After we landed, I finally made my way to the front of the airport. I quickly noticed a big sign that said "Coach Cutler" that the Olympic Committee had made for me. I went to the sign and introduced myself to several representatives saying, "I'm Coach Cutler." After the introductions, they escorted me to Rice University where I met the other coaches. The next 10 days we practiced, played baseball games, ate great meals, went sightseeing, watched the Astros play, and interacted with some major league players and coaches. We thoroughly enjoyed ourselves and I had one of the best times of my life.

My roommate for the next 10 days was Coach Mack Shupe from J.J. Kelly High School in Virginia. He and I became good friends. He ended up winning eight state championships during his coaching career and was an outstanding coach. At the time of the Olympic Festival, however, I had more wins than he did, so I enjoyed giving him a hard time about that. There was a total of 64 baseball players and 12 coaches that the Olympic Committee had selected from all over the United States. In addition to helping the baseball players develop their skills, the committee would pick from this group to determine who would go on to compete in the Olympics in 1988.

On our very first morning, we were given brand new uniforms that we were to wear for our games. We were asked to immediately get dressed in them for the Olympic Festival Opening Ceremony. We were transported from Rice to the Houston Astrodome in a caravan of vans. We arrived to a crowd of over 20,000 fans already sitting in the stands. As one of the coaches for the East Team, I had the honor of being in a procession alongside 3,000 athletes considered the best in the United States with their coaches. Leading the procession was Carl Lewis, winner of several Olympic gold medals in track and field. The festival torch arrived by bicycle, and was then carried by Olympic sprinter Kirk Baptiste and gymnast Kristie Phillips to the platform on the floor of the Astrodome. When they lit the ceremony torch, the festival competition was officially opened. It was just like the Olympic Games Opening Ceremony, after which I understand this was modeled.

We soon had our first practice, held at the Astrodome where the Houston Astros played their Major League Baseball games. Currently the Astros were on the road playing their out-of-town games. For my first coaching task, the head coach told me and Mack Shupe to take the pitchers down to the bullpen to work with them. There were six pitchers on our team and two catchers. When we started to walk down to the bullpen, we noticed there were about 40 to 50 people following us. When we looked closer at the group, we noticed that they all had radar guns. The people were professional baseball scouts. They were here because the baseball players at the Olympic Festival were known to be the best 17- and 18-year-olds in the United States. More specifically, they heard that the East Team had some of the very best pitchers.

Mack and I started out talking to the pitchers and catchers giving introductions and letting them know what the week was all about. We told them to get loosened up and to start out by throwing 30 to 40 pitches in the bullpen. I will never forget how one of the first pitchers entered the bullpen, young Mike Mussina. Mike was from Williamsport, Pennsylvania, and had just graduated from Montoursville Area High School. He had a 24-4 win/loss record with a 0.87 earned run average for his school's baseball team. Mike was drafted from his high school by the Baltimore Orioles, but he chose to attend college at Stanford University instead of signing. He came up to me and said, "Coach, I have been working on a good pitch, a new pitch. I want you to check my fundamentals on this pitch and if you see anything, I want you to give me some suggestions."

I said, "Okay, I will be glad to." When I first saw him pitch in the bullpen, I knew he was special because everything was so smooth. He was about 6 feet tall and 180 pounds. He was throwing close to 90 miles an hour and not even throwing hard for him. After he blazed about 15 pitches, he came up to me and said, "Do you have any suggestions?" I knew I was going to like these guys because they were so coachable and very friendly.

Another pitcher who was in the bullpen with Mike was Willie Banks, who threw even harder than Mussina did. Willie was from Jersey City, New Jersey, and had graduated from St. Anthony High School. During his high school career, he struck out 19 batters of the 21 batters he faced in a seven-inning game on two different occasions. Willie was drafted from his high school by the Minnesota Twins.

One of the catchers in the bullpen was Jesse Levis from Philadelphia. He had just graduated from Northeast High School. Right out of school he was drafted by the Philadelphia Phillies, but decided not to sign on and instead accepted a baseball scholarship from UNC-Chapel Hill.

After all six pitchers had a chance to throw, we had a nice talk. I emphasized what an honor it was for them and the coaches to be at the Olympic Festival. I said as coaches we were there to support and help them. We would be giving suggestions, but they were already excellent players and we did not want to make any drastic changes in a week.

At the end of the practice session, an Olympic Committee representative came down with us and said, "I have somebody I want you guys to meet." We did not know who it was and certainly did not think we would have the opportunity to be meeting any of the Astros' players since they were out of town. To our amazement, the person we were to meet was Nolan Ryan, one of the greatest pitchers of the American League who was later inducted into the Baseball Hall of Fame in 1999. Ryan was currently on the DL, disabled list, due to an injury. He was staying in Houston rehabbing. He told our pitchers and catchers that he would be around until he got off the DL and he would be available to help out in any way.

About four days later, we had a practice scheduled for 4:00 in the afternoon at the Astrodome. The Astros were back in town and were supposed to play following our practice. Word had gotten out that Nolan Ryan was recuperated and expected to pitch, so a crowd started gathering in the stands towards the end of our practice. Around 5:30 p.m., the head coach asked me if I would hit fungo to the infielders. Fungo is hitting balls for fielding practice.

So, I started hitting to the players for fielding practice in the Astrodome, certainly a dream for any baseball coach. I hit balls to the infielders and then to the outfielders. After several minutes, I was ready to bring it home so I hit the ball to the third baseman. When the ball came home to the catcher, Jesse Levis, he looked at me and said, "All right Coach, let's see what you got."

"What do you mean Jesse?" I said.

"I want you to hit a popup straight up in the air," he told me.

To knock the ball straight up in the air for a catcher to practice catching it simulates a pop fly. Hitting a pop up for a catcher is extremely difficult to do if you are standing at home plate.

"Jesse, I'll just throw it up in the air."

"No," he said, "I want you to hit it."

By this time there were about 35,000 people in the stands who were waiting on the Astros, so I was a bit nervous. Nevertheless, I went ahead and took the fungo bat and made a mighty swing. I was saying to myself, "God, just let me hit it straight up in the air." Instead of going straight up, the ball went out toward the scoreboard over the top of the center fielder's head. I heard some laughing in the stands and I assumed it was because of my hit. More determined, I prayed again, "God, just let me hit it straight up in the air." So, I took another swing and the ball did exactly what it was supposed to do. It went straight up in the air and Jesse was there to catch it.

"Coach, you can't do that again can you?" he asked.

Well, I hit another one, also straight up in the air and I was feeling really good. Then the other catcher said, "Coach, are you going to hit me one too?"

"Sure," I said. This time the ball went straight up in the air, once again, and the catcher caught it. I was three for four in front of 35,000 people at Houston Astrodome and thought that was enough.

The team then ran in to where I was, we had a brief talk, and we jogged off to our dressing facility. As we left, the Astros baseball players came into the Astrodome and were getting ready to start their infield. The coach from the Astros then came up to me and had his fungo bat in his hand. He had apparently witnessed my three pop ups. He looked at me and started to hand me his bat and said, "Coach, that was pretty good. Do you want to stay around and hit for me?"

Surprised and yet honored, I said, "No, sorry. I can't do that."

I felt comfortable hitting fungo with the recently graduated high school ballplayers, but I was not ready to hit it with the major league ballplayers. After the team and coaches finished dressing out of our practice clothes, we all went back into the Astrodome and watched the Astros play and Nolan Ryan pitch.

We ended up playing our games at Rice University. We won three out of four of our games, but we did not win the championship. While only the coaches on the championship team progressed to the next level, we did have three players, Mike Mussina, Willie Banks, and Jesse Levis, who did progress.

At the end of the week, after our games and practices, we had a last team meeting. During this time, we signed baseballs. Ever since 1986, I have kept my baseball on my bedroom dresser. Along with the players on the East Team, the baseball has the names of Mike Mussina, Willie Banks, Jesse Levis, and Coach Mack Shupe on it, as well as my name. When I look at the baseball, I think how fortunate it was for an ol' country boy to go to Houston and be associated with three great future major league ballplayers.

When I see Mike Mussina's name, I remember how in 1986 he asked me to check his fundamentals and give him suggestions on his knuckle curveball he was just developing. I was extremely impressed with it, and was not surprised when this became his trade pitch and helped put him in the Baseball Hall of Fame. I am humbled that I was one of the very first to see him perform this very special pitch.

When I see Jesse Levis' name, I remember how in 1986 he asked me to hit a pop up straight up in the air to simulate a fly ball for him to catch. As he caught for the pitchers of the East Team, I was in awe and was not surprised he went on to play professionally for the Cleveland Indians and Milwaukee Brewers. I am humbled that he wanted me to hit fungo with him. He believed I could do the difficult job in front of 35,000 people in the stands watching. When the Astros' coach asked me if I wanted to hit for him, I thought I could not because I would be hitting to Major League Baseball players. But I suppose I had already been doing just that with Levis. Coaching at the Olympic Festival was truly more than a dream come true.

The Best Fishing Ever

There is one thing the Cutlers have in common with each other: they each like to fish. It all started with my father, Joseph Holden Cutler, Sr., or Joe for short. Ever since I can remember, my father had been an avid fisherman and he particularly enjoyed deep sea fishing. That enthusiasm was passed down to my brother and me as well as to the grandchildren. Now that my father was in his late seventies, my brother and I decided we needed to take him on a special deep sea fishing trip. My three sons, who were in their late twenties, wanted to join the adventure.

Our plan was to charter a deep sea fishing boat off Cape Hatteras and fish in the Atlantic Gulf Stream in late October. We knew a fishing boat captain, Rom Whitaker, who sailed out of Cape Hatteras. He had the reputation of being one of the best captains on the East Coast in the United States. The cost for all six of us was just $650 for a full day. Today, in 2021, this same trip would cost close to $2,000.

We had heard that several of the captains were not taking their boats out into the Atlantic because the water was too rough. In case we were still able to go out into the Atlantic this October day, I had mentally prepared myself for the unusual rough water. While during my lifetime I had only been seasick once, I never forgot the experience. In fact, I had been so seasick that one time, I could not fish at all the entire day.

Finally, the day came for our trip and the six Cutlers met the captain and the first mate at 6:00 in the morning at the Hatteras Marina. The captain said we were clear to launch and we were ready to catch some big fish. After leaving the marina, we went out about 200 yards. To my surprise, I remember noticing how calm the water was. The captain and the first mate dropped a large fishing net out about 40 yards to catch some bait fish. The boat then made a circle and they started to bring in the net. When the net reached the boat, we saw that it was full of menhaden fish about 14 inches in length. The net was so full that we had trouble pulling it onto the boat. There were two barrels on deck where we put the fish bait to keep them alive for a long period of time.

After traveling out of sight of land, the captain decided to try out our luck. The first mate baited our lines and we began fishing. Fortunately, the water was still calm. Within a short time, we began catching king mackerel. I mean everybody was catching king mackerel, and big ones too! Some of the mackerel were as large as 15 to 25 pounds. The captain said this was the best fishing he had seen in a month. After fishing for about an hour, the captain decided to go out further.

In the boat, there were two chairs where two people could sit and fish. We gave my father and my brother the honors of sitting in the chairs. The rest of us watched as both of them soon had fish on their lines just within 15 minutes. My father was strapped in his seat and fighting a big one. Several times the fish jumped out of the water and we could see it was a huge blue tuna. After fighting for 20 minutes, my father was pooped and needed help from his grandsons to get the fish aboard. Finally, after fighting for 30 minutes, the blue tuna was close enough for the first mate to help get it aboard. My daddy's tuna was 63 pounds.

In the next hour, we caught bluefin tuna, yellowfin tuna, and more king mackerel. Mike even had the honor of catching the only pelican. The big pelican wanted the mackerel on the end of the fishing line and got itself hooked. It was very difficult bringing in the pelican but at last Mike did. The first mate was able to remove the hook from the bird and send it on its way.

While our arms were extremely tired from fighting the large fish all day long, this was the best fishing any of us had ever experienced. We ended up catching over 700 pounds that day with several fish that were citation size. Interestingly enough, we never made it all the way out to the Gulf Stream. We had no need because the fishing was so good offshore.

When we came back, I made arrangements to have the 700 pounds of fish professionally cleaned. The cost was $200.00 and it was well worth it.

When I got home, I shared the fish with many of my neighbors in Bedford. Having the bluefin and yellowfin tuna was a real delicacy and we all enjoyed it.

This fishing experience was a trip of a lifetime and we still talk about it years later. It was special not only because we caught so many large fish but because we had such calm waters and no one got sick. Most importantly, this was a very special time for my dad. He had the biggest catch of his life and got to spend the day with his two sons and three of his grandsons.

Snow Skiing

Before we had children, Justine and I enjoyed skiing at the Homestead in Hot Springs, Virginia. While we had kept our 1960s ski equipment, we never had time to get away and ski. Finally, when the children were in high school, we ventured out to Wintergreen Resort in the Blue Ridge Mountains and taught the children. They all caught on fast and soon surpassed me.

After Jeff and his best friend, Tommy Field, were in their twenties, they invited me to go skiing with them at Snowshoe, in West Virginia. At the time, I was in great shape having trained for several marathons. What I had not perfected, however, was my skiing. I was proficient on the beginner slope and even the intermediate, but I was certainly not ready for the advanced slope.

Jeff, Tommy, and I were skiing on the intermediate slope. After making the run, though, somehow I got on the wrong ski lift and was headed to the advanced slope. I knew something was wrong when I saw no one else on the ski lift. As soon as I got off the lift and looked down, I could tell for sure I was in the wrong place. The run went straight down for at least half a mile. In addition, the temperature was 18 degrees and I could see severe icy conditions on the slope in front of me. I needed to get off the mountain, but how? I determined that I was not going to be carried out on a stretcher. I knew better than to ski down this advanced and treacherous slope.

So, I did the next best thing, I sat on my rear end and slid down the slope holding my legs and skis up in front of me in the air. I traveled faster than I had ever traveled on skis. While sliding down what seemed like an almost 90-degree angle would be fast enough, the icy conditions increased the speed even more dramatically.

As I made my way down the half mile angle on my rear end, all of a sudden I started to smell something burning. It was my ski pants from all the friction! Once off the "cliff" I started bobbing my way through the small moguls of the run like I was a car on a roller coaster with no brakes. In the end I made it to the bottom of the slope where I saw people again. I bravely got up off my rear, put my feet on the ground still in my skis, and went for the finish line.

A few minutes later I ran into Tommy and Jeff who said, "We were wondering where you were." I started to tell them my story, but some things are really better left unsaid.

As we were leaving the ski area, we saw multiple ambulances taking people to the hospital from having accidents while skiing. I was more than grateful I wasn't being carried out on the stretcher.

Biking Across the
Blue Ridge Mountains

In 1986 I had run four marathons in one year and had injured my left leg. My family had bought me an 18-speed Trek bicycle for me to ride while my leg healed and until I could run again. I soon found a riding buddy who changed my life. In the years to come, we took trips on our bicycles all over the East Coast of the United States and Canada.

My riding buddy was Jackson Overstreet, and he was a unique individual who was in incredible shape for his age. He would later in life walk the entire Appalachian Trail, all 2,190 miles, and ride his bicycle from the state of Oregon to the Atlantic Ocean in 68 days. He was a regular Forrest Gump but highly intelligent. He had a successful career, a funny sense of humor, a wonderful family, and most importantly, he was a strong Christian man.

On our first trip together, we rode from the Peaks of Otter, Virginia, to Front Royal, Virginia. We planned to begin our journey around mile marker 86 on the Blue Ridge Parkway at the Peaks of Otter. We would then ride north for about 85 miles until we picked up Skyline Drive, a public road that runs north to south along the crest of the Blue Ridge Mountains. After getting on Skyline Drive, we would ride 105 miles to Front Royal. Our total miles would be almost 190 and we planned to make this journey in three days. We would fit our bikes with pannier bags on the front and back wheels. In these bags we would carry our tent, sleeping bags, cooking unit, all our food, water, additional clothes, and billfolds with our important cards/ documents.

We left early in the morning heading north on the Blue Ridge Parkway. We soon found that riding on the Blue Ridge Mountains was very difficult because of the change in elevation and the additional weight we were pedaling. As we began our journey northward, the sun shone over the two tall Peaks of Otter warming our backs.

The trek became more strenuous as we began the nine mile climb up Thunder Ridge towards the Radar Base. The Radar Base sits at an elevation of 4,206 feet and was a very important radar installation during the Cold War. Its radar could detect aircraft for hundreds of miles in all directions. It was run by the U.S. Air Force. In 1975, however, the base was deactivated by the Air Force and ownership was transferred to the Federal Aviation Administration (FAA). Today, the base is known as the Bedford FAA Radar Site. Over the years, the equipment was dismantled, with parts still being used by the FAA at first. The Air Force camp was abandoned and leveled. The area that was used for Air Force operations was later reduced with the FAA using a few buildings and other buildings placed into private ownership.

Once we reached the summit, it was all downhill for about 15 miles to the James River. The view was spectacular. At over 4,000 feet one could see northward in the direction of the Shenandoah Valley and westward in the direction of the mountains of West Virginia. I was going so fast downhill that my eyes were watering and it was hard for me to see. My bike was loaded heavy and I could feel it shaking. The faster I went the more I could feel the vibrations.

Jackson just flew off the mountain at 45 miles per hour. I never saw him again until where the Parkway crossed the James River, just north of Big Island. He was waiting for me there. We continued north toward the one tunnel we would go through that was about a quarter of a mile long. We knew tunnels could be dangerous so we had to be extra cautious. Fortunately, we had no incidents. We continued to climb until we reached the top of Afton Mountain just west of Charlottesville. It was at this point where the Blue Ridge Parkway intersects with Interstate 64 and we had finally arrived at the beginning of Skyline Drive. We now only had 105 more miles on the Skyline to complete our journey.

Riding along I could not help but to think about some of the history lessons I had shared with my students explaining to them how these roads were created. The Blue Ridge Parkway and Skyline Drive were built during the Great Depression of the 1930s by the Civilian Conservation Corps (CCC), which was a federal program. The CCC was a part of President Franklin D. Roosevelt's New Deal that not only provided jobs to unemployed, unmarried men, but also preserved and developed the natural resources on rural lands owned by the federal, state, or local governments. The construction work of the CCC took many of its workers high into the Blue Ridge Mountains where the jobs were hard and very dangerous. The Blue Ridge Parkway and Skyline Drive took years to build but provided employment for many people. Like so many others, Jackson and I were now enjoying the hard work of folks who built them.

As we entered Skyline Drive, the first thing we noticed was that the speed limit changed. On the Blue Ridge Parkway, the speed limit had been 45 mph but now on Skyline Drive it was 35 mph. There were many mountains to climb and many curves to navigate on Skyline. We appreciated the lower speed limit for vehicles that might come near us.

We saw many deer on our trip. In fact, one time a deer came out of the forest and ran beside us as we rode down the road for about half the length of a football field before it departed back into the forest. We were just grateful it stayed in its lane and did not try to get in front of us.

We camped at several campgrounds during our trek. On the third night, we camped on Skyline Drive at a place called Big Meadows Campground, which had an elevation of about 3,550 feet. The camp is best known to be a favorite spot for those looking to see a lot of stars in the night sky, but is also well known for its bears. We not only saw signs that said, "Beware of the Bears," but we were personally cautioned by the park ranger about not leaving food around because the black bears frequently visited the campground. After pitching our tent, we took all of our food, extra clothes, and billfolds with our money/identification and bundled the items. We then took the bundle and tied it in a tree about 10 feet off the ground so the items would be out of any bear's reach.

The next morning, we got up early and loaded our tent and sleeping bags on our bikes and headed down the road to a restaurant about 20 miles away for a late breakfast. After about 30 minutes of riding north on the Skyline Drive, we realized we had left our food and supplies still hanging in the tree at Big Meadows.

We laughed and said we were not going back up the mountain to get it. We located a park ranger later that morning and explained to him what happened. He said he would go back to get our bundle of food and supplies and meet us in Front Royal. Later that day we retrieved all of our belongings from the park ranger. We also met our wives who had driven up from Bedford to meet us in Front Royal to take us home.

My first bicycle trip was a highlight in my life. I loved being in the mountains, riding my new bike, camping, seeing the work of the CCC, and being with a good friend. I also realized that I had a lot to learn before our next bike trip.

One Hundred Percent Blocked

As I lay in and out of consciousness at Lynchburg General Hospital, Dr. Kerry, a cardiologist, said to me, "Coach, I can't get through. I can't get through."

Even though I was not fully conscious, I was able to understand that Dr. Kerry was saying I had a 100 percent blocked artery in my heart. As the heart catheterization continued, I learned further that the blockage was inoperable. In other words, no stent could be put in at that location.

Then, at last, I was able to hear some good news. "You have a total blockage, but miraculously, your blood has found its way around the blockage and has been able to continue to the heart to prevent a heart attack."

And then some not so good news from the doctor, "You have several other arteries that are 30 to 40 percent blocked."

After the procedure was completed, I had the opportunity to meet with Dr. Kerry. He immediately started me on a statin and a baby aspirin a day. Most importantly, I will never forget what he said to me, "You are one lucky guy. You pushing yourself to exercise over the years saved your life."

For years I had run four to six miles every day and was always running in road races. I actually ran in four different marathons in one year. To complete one marathon, you must run a total of 26.2 miles, which is not easy. When I hurt my left leg and could not run, I started trekking across the United States and Canada on my bike. As my leg healed, I then started to enter triathlons where I would swim, bike, and run various distances to complete the race. Also, to my advantage, I never smoked tobacco, took drugs, or even drank alcohol, except some homemade wine occasionally from my backyard grape vineyard.

Looking back, I did remember that sometimes when I ran, I would feel extremely winded for the first 10 minutes or so, but then my breathing would improve and I could run long distances. The first time I really knew something was seriously wrong was when I was playing golf in a tournament at the Bedford County Country Club. I was riding on a golf cart and had just gotten out to hit my ball when suddenly I became dizzy and started sweating profusely. I felt like I had never felt before, and it definitely got my attention. Fortunately, the symptoms went away after about 10 minutes, and I was able to finish playing the golf match, so I thought I would be okay.

The next day I was playing the second round of the tournament, and, on the very same hole where I had felt so strangely the day before, the same symptoms reappeared. That evening we had a family dinner and my son, Jeff, who was a paramedic for Carilion, was there. I told him about the two episodes, and we agreed I should go to the doctor the next morning. He also made it clear to me that if I had any trouble during the night, I should go to the emergency room immediately. The next morning, I went to Dr. Buchanan in Bedford. He immediately sent me to see a cardiologist in Lynchburg.

In Lynchburg, they first put me on a treadmill. I was in the room with two nurses and a doctor and was hooked up to all kinds of wires that went to their medical equipment. I was told by the doctor to begin walking on the treadmill and to raise my hand if I had any burning or tightness in my chest. The race began. I started walking and they just kept watching and waiting. Even though the treadmill speed was increasing, my heartbeat would not increase. Finally, they put the treadmill at running speed. My heartbeat finally increased a little but not enough for them to gather data. The doctor then asked me, "Are you on any medicine?" I assured him that I was not. They increased the speed to 7 miles an hour, but my heartbeat only increased a little.

He then said, "We have never had the treadmill turned up so high and had a person's heart to beat so slow." After a good while of waiting for my heartbeat to increase, they gave up and told me to get off the treadmill. The cardiologist then said, "Your treadmill results are amazing, but since you had the two episodes, we are going to still do the heart catheterization."

I am glad the doctor did not just rely on my excellent treadmill test results, and proceeded with the heart catheterization; as I described earlier, he found the 100 percent blocked artery. Over the years I have continued to exercise and take my medicine as prescribed. I am very grateful I have never had any further problems.

I now understand that a body can literally grow new blood vessels as a way to bypass cholesterol-clogged coronary arteries. This is a miracle that happened to me, and it can also happen to others. Exercise can make a big difference.

O Beautiful for Spacious Skies

In 1893, an English professor from Massachusetts, Katharine Bates, rode a horse drawn wagon to the summit of Pikes Peak in the state of Colorado. From an altitude of 14,115 feet, she saw the purple mountains and golden green valleys. A poem called "Pikes Peak" came to mind. Shortly after returning from the mountain, she wrote the words that would later become one of the most loved songs, "America the Beautiful."

Each summer for almost 10 years Justine and I spent two weeks traveling around the U.S. and Canada. My wife and I had purchased a 35-foot Midas motorhome and had invited two good friends, Bobbie and Marion Hargrove, to travel with us.

We had driven across the U.S. and ended up in Colorado. One morning found us at the entrance of Pikes Peak. Before driving up the mountain, you had to check in with the park rangers and obtain permission to take your vehicle on the 10-mile trip to the summit. After letting us drive up the mountain with our motorhome, both of the park rangers smiled when we left and said, "Have fun!"

As we started on our journey up to the summit, the road was paved and we passed many cars that were on their way down. Soon, as we gained altitude, we saw there were no guardrails on the sides of the road. In fact, there was nothing to prevent a vehicle from plummeting off. Nevertheless, we continued up the mountain. At about 8,000 feet, the paved road unexpectedly turned into a dirt road and the driving became even more treacherous. When the cars coming down the mountain passed us, we only had a few feet from the edge to spare. It was a scary sight to look out the window and see a drop of 1,000 feet. The ladies were terrified and were in tears. I told them to close their eyes. That didn't work. At 10,000 feet, we saw snow on the side of the dirt road. The climb up the mountain was so steep our motorhome would not go over 10 to 15 miles per hour. Due to there being no guardrails and being only a few feet from the edge, we prayed we would not meet any cars on the "S" curves. I was on the passenger side taking videos of the sights (when my hands were not shaking). Marion was driving. I noticed that his knuckles were white from gripping the steering wheel so tight. Bobbie and Justine were in the back shaking.

We were then at an elevation of 12,000 feet. There, the road became even steeper with more snow on the mountains, and we no longer saw any trees. We were above the tree line. We continued to barely move up the mountain even though our motorhome had a 420-horsepower engine. The only wildlife we saw was a herd of bighorn sheep. They were playing in the snow and on rocks. They seemed not to have a care in the world.

Finally, we safely reached the top of the mountain. The girls were still shaking as they stepped out. After we calmed ourselves, we were able to take in the view of the magnificent mountains and valleys. We could see for miles as there wasn't a cloud in the sky. "O beautiful for spacious skies." The air was thin and it was very cold. The temperature at the gift shop said 28 degrees. We conveniently spent some time in the shop and then decided we needed to depart.

As we prepared to leave, the park ranger at the top of the peak told us to gear down the motorhome and not to hit our brakes very often. We certainly didn't want to lose our brakes on the mountains so we took the park ranger's advice and geared down. On the way back, we saw several cars that had not geared down and you could smell how their brakes had heated.

The return trip down the mountain in our motorhome was just as frightening as it was going up the mountain. At 5,000 feet, a park ranger stopped each vehicle going down and checked its brakes. We were given an "okay" since we had geared down. We were relieved that our brakes were in good working order.

We made it down the mountain. The girls were still shaking and wanted to get out of the motorhome. As a result, we stopped to get out and to talk to the two park rangers that had checked us in. They were still smiling and said, "We told you guys to have fun!" We soon left the Pikes Peak area and prepared ourselves for the next adventure.

I have never forgotten this frightening trip in a 35-foot motorhome. I have also never forgotten the view. Today, when I hear the song "America the Beautiful," my thoughts go back to our trip up to Pikes Peak and seeing that beautiful spacious sky.

The Great Lakes and a Bicycle for Two

I remember that ever since looking at a map of the Western Hemisphere and seeing the five Great Lakes, I have wanted to take a swim in each one of them. I had this opportunity during one of my trips with Justine and friends Marion and Bobbie Hargrove.

We left Bedford in a motorhome and traveled through West Virginia, Ohio, and then Michigan. Our journey led us to the Mackinac Bridge in the state of Michigan. Big Mac, as known by the locals, is just under five miles long and connects the city of St. Ignace with the village of Mackinaw City. As part of I-75, this bridge ranks 24th in length in the world and is the longest suspension bridge in the Western Hemisphere. While it only takes five to seven minutes to cross it by vehicle, the bridge is a scary place for motorists during wind gusts and storms.

Authorities monitor the weather carefully and close the bridge when there are dangerous conditions. For drivers who are anxious about crossing, there is a Driver Assistance Program available. The workers in this program drive the vehicles of those with high anxiety across. When we crossed Big Mac, it was Marion Hargrove's turn to be our driver. As he had driven many school buses in his lifetime, driving across Big Mac for him was "a piece of cake." Marion showed no signs of anxiety and Justine, Bobbie, and I enjoyed the amazing 200-foot-high view.

After we crossed Big Mac, the Island of Mackinac came into view. This island is about eight miles from land and must be reached by ferry as no vehicles are allowed on it. People come from all over the world to see the island and to taste its famous fudge. Justine and Bobbie wanted to experience the many novelty shops and Marion and I wanted to explore the island along the eight-mile walking and biking road that runs the perimeter of the island. Instead of walking, however, Marion and I decided we would rent a bicycle for two to ride along the pathway. The only problem with this idea was that neither of us had ever ridden a bicycle built for two and we had no idea how hard it would be to maneuver such a bike.

As we started out, we could not keep the bike steady. The people along the pathway who saw us coming cleared out like the parting of the Red Sea. After we got some speed, the bike would settle down, but not until then. I laughed so hard my stomach hurt for hours. Finally, after starting and stopping along the pathway for about three miles, we got the hang of it and no longer had to scare the pedestrians. It did take us a very long time to get back to the area where we were to meet back up with Justine and Bobbie. They had started to worry about us. We were so delayed because of how long it took us to master the bike. After our ride, we all took a carriage ride and visited Fort Mackinac and other historic places.

We took our ferry back and traveled to Sault Ste. Marie, Michigan, where we saw the ships come through the locks. We then traveled through the country visiting each Great Lake. I swam in Lake Michigan and then very quickly in Lake Superior, as it was really cold. We made our way to Lake Huron, Lake Erie, and Lake Ontario. No one else would swim with me but my dream of swimming in each Great Lake was fulfilled, along with the unexpected experience of riding a bicycle built for two.

OBX

Unless you have lived in Eastern Virginia or Eastern North Carolina, you would probably not know what OBX means. OBX is an area that juts out into the Atlantic in northeastern North Carolina just south of the Virginia border. OBX stands for the Outer Banks of North Carolina. To get to the OBX, you must cross a 3½ mile bridge over the Pamlico Sound. Once you cross the bridge, you could go north for 50 miles or south for 100 miles to Cape Hatteras. Along the OBX there are many small towns, rustic villages, and a national park.

People come to this area for different reasons. Many people enjoy the beach; however, OBX is noted for its rough surf and dangerous rip tides. In fact, over the years many ships have sunk off the OBX coast due to the treacherous waters. A 193-foot lighthouse on Hatteras Island is most famous and was actually moved inland over half a mile. Other people come to visit Kitty Hawk where the Wright Brothers made their first flight in 1903 and see the memorial that honors them.

People come to play golf at one of the scenic courses and others come to visit where the movie, *Nights in Rodanthe*, was filmed. Many enjoy chartering a boat and going out in the Oregon Inlet deep sea fishing. Some people especially like walking and hang-gliding off the sand dunes just south of Nags Head. There are many things people do only at OBX, but what Steve Boyer, Bill Boyer, Ricky Falls, and I went to do was fish.

We had come to the OBX for a weekend of fishing near the Oregon Inlet. In 1846, the effects of a hurricane separated Bodie Island from Pea Island forming the inlet. There was a ship called the Oregon that rode out the hurricane in the Pamlico Sound. The crew of the ship told those on the mainland about the inlet's formation. As a result, the inlet was named the

Oregon Inlet after the ship.

For us to get to our fishing area, we had to cross the Herbert C. Bonner Bridge, which as of just a few years ago no longer exists. This magnificent bridge was under three miles long and had a beautiful view looking down on Highway 12 below. The inlet is where all the water from the sound flows into the Atlantic Ocean. This is where fishing boats going to the Atlantic Ocean must pass.

We were going to fish very close to the bridge, just a short distance from the ocean. We had brought over throw nets with us to catch our bait in the sound. The expedition was composed of very experienced fishermen. Steve Boyer, Bill Boyer, Ricky Falls, and yours truly have caught many citation fish in the Maury and James Rivers in Virginia. Soon we were fishing close to the bridge. Steve and Ricky caught some great flounders that were over 25 inches long. Bill and I caught puppy drums about the same size. After fishing from the shore, we decided to walk out close to the main channel. We carried our minnow baskets and walked out about 200 yards from the shore.

Ricky told us that when the tide started coming in the inlet, the fish would be swimming right by us. That sounded great, but I knew the sharks would follow the fish right by us too, so I tried to position myself between the three tall guys. I reasoned that the sharks would go after the big bait first.

After a while, the tide began to come in and we were excited because we could see the small fish jumping out of the water. After catching some nice fish, I hooked a big one. It first began running out towards the ocean and I fought the monster for nearly 20 minutes. I was then able to walk back to shore, but the monster still fought me fiercely. After a good while, I was able to see "it." The monster was over 3½ feet wide. It was a flattened fish in the shape of a disk and had a tapering tail armed on the tip with venom. Its body was flexible and made up of cartilage instead of bones. This monster was a huge stingray.

My three friends were laughing as I got the hook out of its mouth. My good friend Steve, however, took breaks from laughing to remind me to watch out for the tail. Finally, I was able to safely return the stingray back to the water and off it went. We continued to fish and had a great rest of the day. We saw no sharks, but I did learn that stingrays are related to sharks in that they are in the same group because of their having cartilage and no bones for a skeleton.

When we returned to where we had left our cooler, throw net, and other items, I noticed that my throw net was gone. I said that either a crab took it to sea or a human took it home. I really liked that throw net too. We finished up the day cleaning the fish and putting them in a cooler. The next morning, we loaded up and started our 330-mile drive back to Bedford.

It was a fun weekend and we all said we should do it again. We never did, but this weekend trip to the OBX gave us some amazing memories. Someone once said, "A friend is worth a million dollars." I am a very wealthy man.

Deer Antlers

Tom was one of my very good friends. He was first and foremost a fine Christian man who lived out his faith on a daily basis. I knew if I ever needed help with something, he would always be there for me. Justine and I got to know Tom and his wife very well when we started to do some camping with them in Florida. This experience can really bring people together because we got to talk a lot and share stories. One story gave us a good laugh, and some interesting insight.

Tom shared that as he was coming out of Miami, Florida, he and his wife went through a toll booth. Since Tom was a large man at 6'2" in height and around 265 pounds, it was not possible for him to handle the toll while wearing his seatbelt. Unfortunately, the toll booth operator saw that Tom did not have on his seatbelt and immediately reported him. Instantly, as Tom left the toll booth, he was stopped by a female police officer who was about 5'1" and had an attitude. She sternly asked why Tom had not worn his seatbelt. Tom tried to explain about his difficulty and she quickly wrote out a ticket. She then asked to see a copy of his car insurance. Tom explained that while in Virginia he was required to have car insurance, which he did, he was not required to have the card on his person. She wrote Tom another ticket. Lastly, she went to the back of his motorhome where he had proudly displayed his deer antlers. She proceeded to tell him the deer antlers were interfering with the visibility on one of the corners of his license plate. As Tom noticed she was getting ready to write a third ticket, he politely asked if she would not write him a ticket for deer antlers if he would remove them. Fortunately, she did agree to his offer and Tom removed the deer antlers.

Having spent a career as a guard in a state prison, Tom had a lot of experience working with officers and was highly respected. Even though he was just as nice and respectful as he could be to this officer, for some reason she did not like him. Finally, after Tom removed the deer antlers he respectfully asked, "I am just wondering, of all the people you could pull over today, why did you pull me over?"

The officer said with tone, "Sir, when you are in Florida, you WILL follow the laws for the state of Florida."

About a week later on this Florida trip, I was also stopped on the Indian Reservation highway because I was going 65 mph in a 45-mph zone. When the officer notified me of how fast I was going, I apologized profusely and promised I would never go that fast again on this highway. I even told him I would always set my cruise control to 45 mph whenever I came into the area again. My wife, Justine, also entered the conversation restating my promises never to speed again. He let me off with a warning.

So why did Tom get picked on?

I guess they really don't like deer antlers in Florida.

The Triathlon

One of the things on my bucket list was to complete a triathlon. I had run four marathons, but never a triathlon. It was in October on my 70th birthday that I decided I would begin training for one to be held in April of the next year in Lynchburg. While I still had a 100 percent blocked artery, I was told that due to my running, the blood vessels around my heart had multiplied and caused my blood to flow normally. I figured the new training would only make me stronger.

As I began training, I found running and biking to be no problem. What caused me the most difficulty, however, was swimming. Nevertheless, I continued training for the swimming part of the triathlon at the Bedford YMCA and ran and biked like I was used to doing.

In January of that year, Justine and I spent the winter in Lake Placid, Florida. I was able to swim in the resort pool at our camping ground and to bike and run through the area. One day, I decided to vary my training and run some cross country. I found myself in an orange grove and soon heard an angry voice yelling, "What are you doing? This is private property. You are trespassing. Get out of here you blankety blank blank." I quickly turned around and was fortunately able to find my way out of the grove. I later learned that the orange grove was threatened by a disease and being sprayed from tree to tree. If I had continued running from tree to tree, I could have accidentally spread the disease further. I felt horrible about my ending up in the orange grove. In the future, I was more careful and made sure I remained on public property at all times as I trained.

One day, I was playing golf in Florida and suffered extreme sharp pains in my chest. That night I was shopping and had the pains again. The pain was so bad the people around me wanted to call the rescue squad, but I decided to try to tough it out. The next day I called my cardiologist, Dr. Chad Hoyt, in Lynchburg. He sent me to see a doctor in Lake Placid where we were staying. This doctor performed tests and found that my heart was okay, but the muscles around it had become strained because of all the swimming I was doing in the resort pool.

I then spoke again to my cardiologist, Dr. Hoyt. He told me to stop swimming and see if the pain would stop. The doctor was right. The pain stopped and I started limiting my swimming for the next few weeks.

My wife, Justine, and I returned to Virginia in the early spring. I felt I was healed up enough to compete in the triathlon which was coordinated by Tim Groover in Lynchburg and called the Angel Triathlon, held in honor of Groover's daughter, Brittney, who had died in a car accident at age 15 in 2002 while traveling home from Forest Middle School in Bedford County. My daughter Cherie was principal of Staunton River High School in Bedford County from 2000 to 2006. During her tenure, there were several student deaths due to horrible car accidents in the community. After one of these accidents in which several students were killed, Groover appeared at Cherie's office door ready to provide support as someone who could understand the pain and suffering the students and faculty were experiencing. Cherie was touched by his giving heart in the midst of his own suffering. It was an honor for me to support the work of Groover, who had lost, and yet given so much.

The Angel Triathlon began with a pool sprint of about 300 meters at the local YMCA. This was the first time I had ever swum in a pool with lanes. I found it to be similar to swimming in the ocean because there were so many waves from all the people. The swim was followed by a 30-mile bike trip. The Lynchburg YMCA was located on a hill overlooking the James River, so I thoroughly enjoyed coasting down the hill, crossing the bridge over the James, and heading down River Road toward Amherst. I had fun passing a lot of people but allowed my senses to get a hold of me and I slowed down so I could save my strength for the final run. At the halfway mark of the bike ride, the journey took me around a 10-foot angel in the middle of the road. Participants had to ride full circle around the angel and then head back to Lynchburg.

When I arrived back in the hill city, I had to take on the large hill I had enjoyed coasting down which led me back to the Lynchburg YMCA. The ride was really tough, but I made it to the top.

I soon began my 3.1-mile run. Fortunately, the run was back downhill to the river, continuing for about two more miles then uphill to the finish line. I had lots of experience with running hills, but this was much tougher because I had already swum 300 meters and ridden my bike for 30 miles.

I soon found a friendly face in the crowd. My son, Mike, found me about a half mile to the finish line. He encouraged me and I was able to gain new strength. I finally made it. I was pretty tired, but happy that I finished. I was even happier, however, that I came second in my age group and received a medal.

I could now mark the triathlon off my bucket list. Nevertheless, I completed the event the next year and was even 30 minutes faster. My triathlon days were over.

Fore

Golf has been played for a long time. Since 1861, when Tommy Morris, the first young golf prodigy, won the first of his four British Open Championships at St. Andrews, Scotland, much has changed in the sport, including balls, clubs, dress, and golf courses. I have been playing golf for over 60 years and have never won a major championship. In fact, I have never won any championships. I play golf for the love of the game and the fellowship with others.

Golf can be a lot of fun, but it can also be very humbling. I have witnessed some very unusual occurrences on the golf course. Some are hard to believe, but I promise you, they actually happened.

I was once playing in a senior tournament at the Bedford Country Club. On the first hole, I drove my tee shot into the woods and went to look for my ball. While I never found it, a very aggressive swarm of yellow jackets found me. I took off running as fast as I could to get out of the woods to escape the angry swarm, but the yellow jackets continued to chase me clear down the fairway of the first hole. I had on Bermuda shorts and the yellow jackets stung me repeatedly on both of my legs.

Finally, after I had run, jumped, and hopped for about 50 yards down the fairway, the yellow jackets retreated. The men in my foursome doubled over with laughter as they watched me bouncing down the fairway also making some loud verbal noises. I ended up with stings on both of my calves and had to go to the club house for some ice. Somehow, I finished playing the tournament, but my legs hurt for a good two days.

There is a hole at the Bedford Country Club that has a pond close to the green. I hit my tee shot right next to the pond. Since I did not have a clear shot to the green, I decided to just hit the ball back into the fairway where I could have a better next shot. To reach my goal, I had to take off my shoes and socks, stand in the water with one leg, and hit the ball back into the fairway. I missed the ball and fell backward straight into the lake. As I climbed out of the water, I could hear everyone laughing loudly. To make matters worse, as I had fallen backward into the lake, my shoe had moved my ball, so I had to take an unplayable drop. I was finally back in the fairway, but ended up with an eight on the par four hole, which was not what I had wanted to do.

I was playing with a very good golfer, Cecil Camden, in the Member Guest Tournament at the Bedford Country Club. On the par five hole, Cecil hit a beautiful 220-yard drive, but the ball ended up under a tree. As Cecil and I came up to his ball, he confidently told me to watch his next shot. He took out his driver and swung at the ball that flew out from behind the tree, but about 50 yards right behind the ball came the head of Cecil's driver. In addition to hitting his ball, Cecil had also whacked the tree with his driver. He was standing there looking at his ball in the fairway along with the head of his driver right next to the ball while he held what was left of his golf club. We won our flight that weekend, which was $100.00 each, but Cecil had to pay a lot more to replace his driver.

I have played many rounds of golf with my golfing friend, Steve Boyer. Steve is a big man. He is about 6'5" and weighs about 240 pounds. Steve can hit some spectacular shots, but every now and then he has trouble with hooking his drive. The par four hole at the club runs parallel to Route 43, which runs right to the Blue Ridge Parkway. One day, Steve had a tough time on this hole. Instead of hitting the ball straight he hooked it toward the highway. It just so happened that a car was coming south toward Bedford and to our astonishment, the golf ball hit the windshield of the car completely shattering it. The lady who was driving the car had to immediately stop the car on the side of the road. To make matters worse, Steve soon recognized the very upset woman. At the time, Steve was the principal of Liberty High School and she was a worker in the school cafeteria. After ensuring the woman was not injured, Steve told her he would pay for everything and would drive her home. The lady, however, insisted that she could drive home and we saw her start down the road with her head out the window because she could not see out of her front windshield. Steve called her later that evening to make sure she was all right and learned she had already made arrangements to get the windshield to her car fixed. He promised her he would pay for the repairs to her car. Unfortunately, Steve's insurance would not cover the accident because the company said he had not hit the ball into the road on purpose and he was not drinking alcohol. Of course, Steve still paid for the repair of the shattered windshield and most importantly his cafeteria worker was safe and forgave him.

Dallas Key is a good golfer, sometimes. On one winter day, he was playing on the hole next to the small pond at the Bedford Country Club. Dallas' drive landed right next to the pond. He started down the bank in the golf cart, but he apparently did not notice that the ground was frozen and icy. To my amazement, the golf cart began to gently slide towards the water. Dallas frantically tried to stop but to no avail. The golf cart slid right into the pond and landed with the front submerged and its back end up in the air with Dallas' golf clubs still visible. Unhurt by the incident, he got out, collected his golf clubs out of the partially sunken cart and finished the round of golf. The golf cart remained in the pond for three days until it could be safely removed. As a good sport, Dallas paid the Bedford Country Club to have it replaced.

I was playing once with my very good friend Terry Tarrence from Hale, Michigan, who is an excellent golfer. It was in the winter time and we were playing at a course in Lake Placid. Terry was having a fine round of golf until he came to the par three. He hit his five iron into the bunker on the left and I hit my drive to the right. We did not know it, but they had just dumped a new load of sand in his bunker. I could not see Terry across the green, but I could see the sand flying in the air like a cloud of smoke. It took Terry nine shots to get out of the trap. Every time I saw sand come flying out, I was laughing harder. I remember laughing so hard, my stomach muscles cramped and I had tears in my eyes. Terry eventually made it out and two-putted for an 11 on a par three. Terry, however, ended up shooting an 86 on 18 holes, which was not bad for taking an 11 on one hole.

In south Florida they have a lot of alligators on the grounds and even on the golf courses. Some gators can reach a length of 10 feet. There are stories of people losing arms to these large alligators when they get too close to the water. Fortunately, when the alligators get too big, most golf courses move them to a big lake. I was playing on one of the courses in South Florida that happened to have many ponds with some big boy alligators. On one hole I hit my driver close to the water. As I drove my cart to the ball, I saw a big alligator slide into the water about 20 yards off. I parked my cart and got ready to hit my second shot 120 yards from the green. Just as I was getting ready to hit my shot, I heard my playing partner yell, "Jim, here he comes!" I knew it was that massive alligator I had just seen slither into the water. I took off running to get into my golf cart that was 10 yards away. As I approached it, I could hear my friend laughing. The alligator was still in the pond, but I didn't know that. I told him I would get even with him. I did later.

Squeaky Wooldridge is one of our super seniors at the Bedford Country Club. There is a hole that you hit into the bottom of the fairway and the green sits at the top of the hill to the right. There is a creek on the left that runs into a pond. Squeaky hit a good shot into the fairway and was driving his golf cart down a long steep cart path to his ball. He reached over to pick up a ball but fell out of the cart. I saw Squeaky roll several times down the hill before he stopped. The golf cart with his clubs did not stop and even picked up speed as it flew halfway across the creek and stopped but continued to sink. Squeaky rushed to the cart and was able to get his clubs out before it disappeared. He went back to the club house, reported the incident, got another golf cart and finished his round. The golf supervisor ended up getting a large tractor and chain and was finally able to pull the cart out of the water.

One morning I was playing another round of golf with my good friend, Steve Boyer, also at the club. He was still having trouble with hooking his drives. We were back on the par four hole that ran along the busy Route 43. Steve hit his drive off the tee and once again hooked it into the road. This time, however, a large logging truck was going north toward the Peaks of Otter. Steve's golf ball hit the back of the truck. The truck never stopped but continued going up the road. The next thing we saw was the golf ball flying back toward the fairway after hitting the logging truck. The golf ball ended up 230 yards from the tee in the fairway. Steve hit the ball again and it landed on the green. Steve then two-putted for a magnificent par. I called that par a miracle par.

Marion Hargrove, another golfing buddy of mine, was pulling a three-wheel pull golf cart with his clubs on it as he played at the Bedford Country Club. He parked his cart next to the green, but the cart had a mind of its own and headed down the hill. Below the green was a large pond. I was walking to reach my ball when all of a sudden, I saw Marion's cart fly down the hill. It flew past me and continued across the fairway traveling very fast and flying into the big pond, completely disappearing. The next thing I saw was Marion coming down the hill trying to find his three-wheel pull golf cart. He then saw a boat along the bank of the pond. Marion and I boarded the boat and floated to where we thought his clubs were. He was somehow able to grab his golf bag with his clubs in them and I paddled the boat back to shore. All 14 golf clubs were safely rescued, but his golf bag was full of water. No problem, Marion simply turned his golf bag upside down, dumped the water out of the bag, and walked back to the hole he had left and continued his golf game. Our foursome had a hard time concentrating on the rest of the round because every time we would get ready to hit our balls, we would see Marion in our minds dumping the water out of his golf bag. Once again, I laughed until my stomach hurt and my eyes filled with tears.

Like I said, I have never won any championships playing golf. So why do I play? I play golf for the love of the game and the fellowship with others.

Christmas Angels Restore Vision

It was two days before Christmas, and I was finishing up my shopping. About 4:30 p.m. I was driving home. I noticed, out of the blue, a bright flash in my left eye. The flash was so bright that I thought it was lightning outside. When I returned to my home in Bedford, I noticed what looked like cobwebs and floaters in my left eye. It did not hurt, but for the rest of the night the cobwebs and floaters continued.

The next day was Friday and Christmas Eve, the time of our annual tradition to steam 10 pounds of shrimp and have the whole Cutler family, children and grandchildren, come to our home and eat lots of shrimp for about two hours. It was one of the highlights of Christmas.

About 11:30 a.m. on Friday, my eye was no better and I thought I should give Dr. Dave Gladwell a phone call about it. For many years I had known Dave and he had worked with me to prescribe glasses and contact lenses for me. After I described the problem, he said it should be okay but to check with him on Monday after Christmas. Just 15 minutes later, my phone rang and it was Dr. Gladwell. He said he had talked to Dr. Gene Moss, a Cornea Specialist, and he had agreed to see me after he saw his patients that afternoon.

I arrived about 4:30 p.m. at Dr. Moss's office, which was in Bedford. By this time, everyone had left the office to spend time with their families on Christmas Eve. After dilating both eyes and completing the exam, Dr. Moss looked at me and said, "Coach, you have a detached retina." It was around 5:00 and I told Dr. Moss I would come back to see him Monday. To my surprise he said, "You need emergency surgery on your eye now or you will lose your vision." Dr. Moss then immediately called Dr. Robert Vogel, a Retina Surgeon. Dr. Vogel said he would meet us in the office in Lynchburg at 5:30 p.m. I followed Dr. Moss to the Piedmont Eye Center in Lynchburg and Dr. Vogel soon arrived. He had on blue jeans, a t-shirt, and flip flops. Obviously, he had come from home and had already started his Christmas vacation. The office was completely empty. There was no one there except for these two doctors and me.

Dr. Vogel examined me and then said, "I will have to do emergency surgery to save your eye." Dr. Moss, who had been with me this entire time, assisted Dr. Vogel with the surgery as there was no other staff. I was in great care. I had a Retina Surgeon and a Cornea Surgeon double teaming me to save my eye on this Christmas Eve.

After the procedure, Dr. Vogel told me the laser surgery was successful and told me to come see him in a week. Dr. Moss told me I was in good hands and went home to spend Christmas with his family.

As Dr. Vogel and I were leaving the office, he looked at me and said, "Coach, could I borrow a $20.00 bill? I told my wife I would bring home a bottle of wine for dinner and I left in such a hurry I forgot my billfold."

I was only too happy to give Dr. Vogel the $20.00 bill in my billfold. After I gave him the money, I went to my car. I did not tell him I was by myself and had to drive back to Bedford. I thought I could make the trip, but between the dilation and numbing medicine, I was feeling strange and having difficulty seeing to drive. I got as far as Forest and pulled over. I called my daughter and her husband, Cherie and David, to come and get me. Cherie drove me home and David drove my car home.

That night the family had gathered at 8:00 p.m. for supper because they knew I would be late. For the first time, I could not eat a lot of shrimp, but my eye was saved. Dr. Vogel and Dr. Moss had gone the extra mile for me on Christmas Eve, and I am thankful for them.

On my return visit to Dr. Vogel's office, he had his assistant give me a $20.00 bill from him to pay me back. Apparently, Vogel had shared with his assistant what had happened, and we had a good laugh. For several years, whenever I saw Dr. Moss for my checkups, we always had a good laugh about the $20.00 too.

That Christmas, I received a gift money cannot buy, my eyesight. God sent these two special Christmas angels, and I will always be grateful.

The Long Goodbye

Justine and I were married for over 53 years. During our 38th year of marriage, when Justine was almost 60, she was diagnosed with highly aggressive stage 3 breast cancer. The diagnosis was shocking to us, as she had never missed her annual doctor's appointment.

My four children, their wives, and I quickly prayed for her as she went through her surgery, chemotherapy, and radiation. Before her chemotherapy treatments, the family gathered at the house, circled her with their love, and one by one prayed for her. Justine kept her Bible near her reading it each day and focusing on God's peace during this storm.

During this time, Justine never cried or was cross but was courageous and positive. She battled her illness with grace and dignity and led her life as normally as possible. After her diagnosis, I taught and coached for five more years. Despite her illness, she continued to be by my side coming to nearly all my baseball games. In fact, out of all of my varsity baseball games that I coached at Bedford High School and Liberty High School, Justine only missed one game, and that was due to a medical treatment. I credit the success I achieved, and my 513 wins as a coach, to her support.

Justine was a graduate of Longwood College and was a dedicated educator. She taught in Bedford County Public Schools for over 30 years. She taught fifth grade at Liberty Academy, English 8 and 9 at Bedford High School, English 8 and 9 at Montvale High School, and English and Drama at Liberty. She was certified to teach English, Theatre, French, History, and Speech/Public Speaking. One of her proudest accomplishments was directing the musical *Oklahoma* at Liberty in 1980, which played to a packed auditorium for three nights.

My wife loved to play golf and was a member of the Ladies Golf Association of the Bedford Country Club. She played in tournaments in Virginia and Florida and achieved a hole in one at the Bedford Country Club. She also loved to travel with me during our summers throughout the United States, Canada, and Mexico. She especially loved to round dance, and was an expert at it, even teaching it to others. She also enjoyed square dancing, bowling, and playing games with family and friends. She loved music and played the piano and organ. She was a great cook and an excellent photographer. She loved her flowers, especially daylilies and caladiums. Justine loved to knit, cross stitch, and embroider, and taught these skills to her granddaughters. My wonderful wife loved God, her family, and others.

The treatments Justine had for the cancer seemed to work for several years. Her oncologist even referred to her as her miracle patient. Then, the unthinkable happened, and the breast cancer returned in 2012, but in her back. During the winter of 2014, she seemed to be progressing nicely and her oncologist made arrangements for her to take her treatments in Florida.

A few days after her first treatment there, we went square dancing.

I remember that last dance.

She looked beautiful and kept smiling at me.

Unfortunately, just a few days later, her situation grew worse. She became so weak she had to be hospitalized. The doctors there gave up on her and she was sent to hospice. I wanted to bring her home, but she was too weak. All four children traveled from Virginia to Florida to be with her. During this time, we prayed together, sang hymns, laughed, and cried. On March 1, 2014, Justine passed into the next life. God had given us 16 extra years with her after her stage 3 diagnosis and we were grateful. The void I still felt, however, was unspeakable and something happened to me. I shook uncontrollably at the moment of her death and was in shock. I had to have some medication. While my faith was strong and I knew I would see her again, I felt lost without her.

On our drive home from Florida, the children and I stopped at Folly Beach in South Carolina, near where my granddaughter Alison and her husband Alex live. It was a cold, cloudy March day, but we all walked on the beach and out on the pier. Justine had been such a big part of all of our lives.

We now had to learn to move forward, but I struggled.

Death is truly the enemy of God's love. It is as Jesus said in John 16:33, "In this world you will have tribulation," but there is coming a day when there will be no more death and all tears will be wiped away.

> *"And God will wipe away every tear from their eyes; there shall be no more death, nor sorrow, nor crying. There shall be no more pain, for the former things have passed away."*
> *Revelation 21:4*

An Honorary Navy SEAL Award

I had been head baseball coach at Liberty for about 23 years. Our teams had been very successful winning many championships and were always one of the best teams in the state. In the early 1980s, a young man, Eddie Hiner, approached me one day and wanted to try out for the varsity baseball team. He was big for a freshman, nearly 6' tall and weighing around 170 pounds. Eddie had recently moved to Montvale, Virginia, living with his widowed grandmother after his mother had a nervous breakdown, and he was attending Liberty High School.

I told Eddie, "Of course you can try out for the team," but I thought to myself he probably would not make it. I was, however, surprised by the way this freshman hit, threw, and conducted himself at tryouts. As a result, I brought Eddie into the coaches' office and started talking to him. He had his head down and was getting ready for the bad news that I was sending him to the junior varsity, but to his surprise, I shared with him that I was going to keep him on the varsity. Years later he would tell me that he cried all the way home because he had made the team.

When I saw Eddie play in his first game, I knew he was a special person. He was a hard worker and had earned himself a spot as a starting player. His first time at bat, he struck out. I spoke to him and told him to keep his head up. His next time at bat, he hit a home run against a pitcher who would later play AAA Professional Baseball. Eddie ended up with three hits that day. He knew how not to give up and how to perform under pressure.

During the course of the next four years, Eddie Hiner led our team to the Regional tournament every year. He led the district in home runs and runs batted in and had the highest batting average. He became one of the best left-handed pitchers in the area. His senior year, he was selected First Team All-State and played in the Virginia High School League All Star Game. That year he had a batting average of .546. Eddie's batting average remains the highest in the 56 years of baseball at Liberty High School.

I was able to help Eddie get a scholarship to Virginia Commonwealth University in Richmond. He played four years there. During those four years Eddie had an outstanding baseball career and had the opportunity to play in two College Regional World Series. Eddie graduated with a degree in business. After graduation, he applied for Navy SEAL training and was accepted. Out of 150 candidates in his 1992 class, only 10 completed the training. Eddie was one of the 10. He deployed to Afghanistan, Iraq, and other places. He went on hundreds of combat missions and earned two Bronze Stars for valor and leadership. Eddie then went to graduate school at USD (University of San Diego) and began leading basic and advanced training for SEALs throughout the country as Lieutenant Commander. Then, after 20 years of service, Eddie retired as a Lieutenant Commander and decorated combat veteran. In his retirement, he wrote the book, *First, Fast, Fearless: How to Lead Like a Navy SEAL*, which made the *Los Angeles Times* best sellers list.

Liberty High School had begun a Sports Hall of Fame and wanted to induct Eddie. In January 2016, he returned to Bedford and was not only inducted, but gave the keynote speech. The day before the induction, Eddie visited Liberty and spoke to over 1,000 students in an assembly. As a part of his presentation, he talked about his years as a student at Liberty and how the teachers and coaches had influenced his life. As he spoke, he connected with the students and you could have heard a pin drop. At the end of his presentation, the students and staff all rose to their feet and gave him a standing ovation.

On the Saturday night of the induction ceremony, about 300 people were there. Eddie spoke for about 20 minutes. At the end of his talk, he said he would like to do one more thing. He then walked back to where I was sitting and asked me to stand up. He took the Poseidon Navy SEAL Medal off his jacket and pinned it on my jacket and then hit the medal three times (a Navy SEAL tradition). He said, "Coach, if it wasn't for you, I would not be where I am today. I love you and you are now an Honorary Navy SEAL." There was not a dry eye in the room.

I had the privilege of coaching baseball for 46 years and received many awards like being inducted into the Virginia High School League Hall of Fame and the Salem-Roanoke Baseball Hall of Fame, but this award, from Retired Lieutenant Commander Navy SEAL Ed Hiner, brought tears to my eyes. Even today I get teary-eyed reliving the moment Eddie put the pin on my jacket. After all, it was because of people like Brian "Eddie" Hiner that I earned the many awards given to me. Eddie had his second book come out in April 2021, *GUTS: Greatness Under Tremendous Stress*. I could not wait to read it. He even mentioned me in his Preface.

A New Song

My entire life I have loved to sing. Hymns and old songs are my favorites. Over the years I was in several quartets, but I always sang in choirs. In high school I sang in the church choir in Richlands. Later when I moved to Bedford to begin my teaching and coaching career, I sang in the church choir at Main Street United Methodist Church and at Word of Life Church. Even during the winter months when visiting Florida, I sang in the church choir there. In all of my adult life, and in the months leading up to my cancer diagnosis, I would go to our piano to play and sing for an hour each night. Singing was more than just a part of my daily routine; it was something that brought me joy. My granddaughter, Alison, recently told me that she can still hear my voice singing "Silent Night" in German each Christmas. Maybe she will teach it to my great grandsons someday.

One thing that disrupted this routine was when I developed laryngitis. I remember I had just walked nine holes of golf at the Bedford Country Club and afterwards noticed these symptoms of laryngitis for three days, so I decided to visit my local physician, Dr. Kurt Hubach. After ruling out allergies and acid reflux, Dr. Hubach referred me to an Ear Nose and Throat (ENT) specialist, Dr. Jay Cline in Lynchburg. After running several tests, Dr. Cline told me I had a mass on my lung and wanted me to see a pulmonary doctor, Dr. John Plankeel, also in Lynchburg. Dr. Plankeel ordered a scan and biopsy of the tumor in my lungs, which was done at Lynchburg General Hospital.

It was the following week when I got the diagnosis. My son Jeff, who is a paramedic, came with me to meet with Dr. Plankeel and to hear the review of the scans and biopsy results. During this appointment, Dr. Plankeel told me I had stage 4 lung cancer and he was going to send me to the Cancer Center to meet with an oncologist. The doctor also told me that stage 4 cancer was not curable, but could be treatable. To my surprise, the scan revealed I had cancer in both lungs, as well as in my liver and bones (lower spine and left hip). The cancer in my lungs was pushing on the nerve that leads to the vocal cords, preventing one cord from working. This was the cause of my laryngitis and what prevented me from talking above a whisper. Fortunately, the doctor ordered an MRI of the brain and called me the very next day telling me the good news that the cancer had not moved into the brain.

The next week I met with a doctor new to the Cancer Center, Dr. Mahmood Rasheed, who was very good and thorough. He took time to explain everything to me and my new wife. Together we mapped out my treatment over the next year. I was to take two chemotherapy drugs and one immunotherapy drug every three weeks via intravenous administration. After four treatments we would have a scan and see how the cancer reacted to this treatment plan. Dr. Rasheed was very optimistic, but cautious. Dr. Rasheed told me he thought this treatment plan could help me talk better, but that I would probably never sing again.

Starting chemotherapy was very challenging, but one of the hardest parts of dealing with the cancer was that I could not talk above a whisper. I could not yell, scream, or sing. I could still play the piano, but singing was out of the picture. I missed singing more than I realized I would. What I needed was a miracle, and we all prayed for one. I finally accepted that I may never sing again here on this Earth, but one day I will be singing with the angels in the most magnificent choir ever assembled, God's choir in Heaven.

I saw a movie years ago called *I Can Only Imagine*. How true those words have become to me now. These words have given me hope because I can only imagine what it will be like to sing in Heaven. I will not have any trouble hitting the A above middle C in the Hallelujah Chorus. I am sure God can find a place for me, and I look forward to singing in the great choir in the presence of God. Until God calls me to join His choir, I will continue living my life to the fullest, praying and praising God.

It may not be with a loud voice that is audible to other human ears, but it will be a new song to God from my heart.

"Sing to the Lord a new song."
Psalm 96:1

Postscript

Learning from the Best
by Cherie Cutler Whitehurst

In 1975, my father came home and announced he was going to start coaching the Liberty High School girls' basketball team since they had no coach. My ears perked up immediately. "I am not a basketball player," I thought, "but I just may want to get in on this."

I began to map out my plan. "Obviously," I plotted, "I cannot start playing on his varsity team. I am going to have to work for it." I would first make the j.v. team, and then work my way up to varsity where I would watch him coach.

The time finally came in my tenth-grade year when I earned my place on my father's varsity team. Most of the girls were older and I felt a bit awkward. I knew I would probably not see much playing time, so my goal was to practice with the first string as hard as I could and help them be the best they could be.

The whistle blew and we lined up for the talk. After the introductions and a list of team expectations and practice procedures, my father said something to the girls I found unexpected: "Most importantly, we are here to have fun." Then he blew the whistle again and he said, "We are starting out with the fundamentals. You cannot play basketball if you cannot pivot, dribble with your head up, shoot, or rebound."

As the drills began, I saw a stark contrast in the performance of the girls with whom he had worked the previous year. These athletes were smoother, faster, and much more knowledgeable and coordinated. I welcomed their friendly smiles when they looked at me learning the new moves. Looking back, they were very patient with the new players.

The pace of the practices picked up as we started to learn more fundamentals like passing and boxing out, along with offensive and defensive basic formations. Then, the day came when we learned our swing offense. As my father coached, I began to see the court open up in geometric shapes and the athletes maneuvering on the court like chess pieces but with the responsibility of working to move the whole team forward like a machine.

After we mastered the swing, my father taught multiple variations of it that would keep our opponents guessing. I saw him polishing team moves by getting his athletes to play in a rhythm that was quick and hard to follow if you did not know the plan. My father was right; this was fun.

We progressed still further learning offensive man-to-man plays that we were taught to alternate with our swing offense based on our scoring or not. In defense, we mastered the basic formations of the zone and man-to-man, and their variations. We learned how to half court and full court press, how to sag, and how to put the clamp on the ball, or double team it. The real fun came when we learned how to execute fast breaks. I watched my father develop the talents and skills of these athletes, who at one time did not even know how to pivot. I especially liked learning the fundamentals and using those new skills to make the first string have to practice harder. The best of all was being a part of a real team, and especially my father's team.

The preseason was over, and it was game time. My dad had fun teaching us to be stars. For each pregame we had a spectacular routine. We ran out of the locker room in single file and headed toward the basket. The captain dribbled the ball towards the goal with the rest of the team still in a single file line. Then the captain jumped high and tapped the ball with her fingertips on the right side of the backboard. The captain kept moving with the girl behind her taking the same action. We ended up in a circle one by one practicing our jumping, speed, coordination, and ability to control the ball in a quick second while having to work as a team. The team had become *so* good at this maneuver that we were able to go fast and it was a rarity that the ball was ever dropped. The crowd cheered and the other teams paused to watch. We then moved to the star passing drills, and after several other drills, the layups. My father had made us look like the best team in the district just in our pregame warmups.

Needless to say, we ended up with an outstanding season. We finished the regular season with only two losses. We won the regular season and the district tournament. We went on to regionals. In this game, my father was able to put me in for a few minutes. At 5'4" and 124 pounds, I played on the wing and had an outside shot that today would be a three pointer. As the swing moved, I found myself open and I took the outside shot making two points for the team in a regional game. I had surpassed what I thought I could do.

We won the regionals and went on to play in the state playoffs. In those days, girls' basketball teams were not grouped by the size of the school. Even though Liberty High School was classified as an AA school according to our size, we would have to play this bigger AAA school. When I first saw the other team, I noticed how tall and muscular each girl was. Our tallest and strongest girls could not even compare despite how quick they were.

Our team played hard and my father coached hard, but we were not able to pull this game off. I had not seen my father lose many games and I was curious how he would handle this loss. While some of the girls were in tears, I watched him start pointing out one by one the many things that the girls did well. He spoke gently and like a father. He spoke inspirationally and motivationally. He made us all feel good about ourselves, and he reminded us of all that we had accomplished. His last words were, "Hey, we had fun, didn't we?"

In my early career as a teacher, I had the opportunity to coach girls' basketball at Forest Middle School in Bedford County. I ran the practices just as I had watched my father run them. I taught these girls the same basic plays my father had taught. I was not comparable to my father, but we only lost one game.

I did not coach long because I went into school administration becoming an assistant principal and taking a turn at being principal in two of Bedford County's high schools, Staunton River and Liberty. I was known as someone who could turn a school around improving the student achievement, discipline, and culture. I then became the Assistant Superintendent and Deputy Superintendent for the county. In all of the training I had for these jobs, including my doctorate, my most important training was what I had on the basketball court at Liberty from my father in the 1970s. He taught me about being an important part of a team and how to work hard, inspire, motivate, take a stand for what is right, and most importantly, treat each person with dignity, respect, and care.

There are many other ball players of my father's who went on to become teachers and coaches including Jim Whorley, Kelly Russell, Jim Thacker, Billy Catron, Barry Gordon, Eddie Burnette, Stewart Grant, Mike Thompson, and Michael Camden to name just a few. I have often wondered if their teaching and coaching were as positively influenced by my father as mine were.

Addenda: Interesting Facts About Jim Cutler

- Swam in all five Great Lakes in one summer
- Won $5,000 in the VA Lottery Pick 4, 7777 (only time those numbers came up)
- Ran up and down the Washington Monument as a senior in high school
- Rode bike on the entire Blue Ridge Parkway and Skyline Drive
- Swam in the Great Salt Lake
- Rode around the Daytona Speedway at 80 mph
- Took piano lessons as a child
- Took organ lessons later in life
- Sang bass in a gospel quartet
- Played golf at St. George, UT, on a desert course when the temperature was 106 degrees
- Rode a "bike for two" around Mackinac Island, MI
- Hit a golf ball over half a mile in Colorado where the elevation was 12,000 feet
- Rode in a speed boat at Smith Mountain Lake over 110 mph
- Had the honor of coaching all four of my children in a varsity sport at LHS
- Surfed down a 100-foot sand dune in New Mexico, White Sands National Park
- In 46 years of coaching, only thrown out of one game (a little league game while coaching sons in Big Island, VA)
- Loved to round dance and square dance with my wife, Justine
- Visited the Grand Ole Opry once in Nashville

- Once won $10,000 on a slot machine in a Casino
- Raised honey bees
- Had over 100 varieties of daylilies planted in yard
- Teamed on many Emmaus Walks
- Got a ticket for not wearing seat belt after a varsity baseball game
- Panned for gold in Colorado
- Rode bike along the North Rim of Grand Canyon
- Caught a yellowfin tuna over 50 pounds in the Gulf Stream off Cape Hatteras, NC
- Watched son, Jeff, catch a 6½ pound rainbow trout in VA
- Once ran out of gas twice in the same day
- Canned over 50 quarts of green beans one summer from own garden
- Prayed each night and often read Bible
- Inducted into three Hall of Fames
- Drove from Bedford, VA, to Lake Placid, FL, in 15½ hours (820 miles)
- Had team pray before every game coached
- Honored by the VA Assembly
- Served as Grand Marshall of the Christmas Parade in Bedford, VA
- Walked down Bourbon Street and the French Quarter in New Orleans one night with son, Michael
- Had a private tour of Fenway Park in Boston
- Never smoked a cigarette or used any tobacco product
- Had a pet crow named Smokestack
- Lived across the street from a bootlegger in Southwest VA who went to prison
- Was almost killed when a coal train caught me on a railroad bridge in Cedar Bluff
- Loved to water and snow ski
- Played golf with a man from Japan who ran after hitting the ball on every shot
- Rode around New York City in December for three hours looking

for Rockefeller Center

- Owned a motorcycle and drove it to school for several years
- Completed several triathlons with a 100 percent blocked artery
- Worked at a coal tipple
- Had a speech impediment as a young child
- Began senior year at Richlands High School at 15 years old
- As a freshman at Hampden-Sydney College played three sports
- Sang with many choral societies in VA and FL
- Minored in Spanish at Hampden-Sydney College
- Grandfather Isaac C. Boyd elected to the House of Delegates in VA for several terms
- Rode bicycle over 40 mph downhill on Blue Ridge Parkway
- Had a bicycle accident in the Bedford Memorial Hospital Parking Lot (walked into ER and they had to give me stitches and treat my broken ribs)
- At one time, had more wins than any high school baseball coach in VA (513)
- Favorite book in the Bible was 1 Corinthians
- Mother was an elementary school teacher
- When growing up father had a pet monkey
- Had a small vineyard in yard and made homemade wine
- Had a German Shephard who stole neighbors' milk after it was delivered by milk man
- Had a student at Liberty High School who went streaking through the hallways in the 1970s
- Purchased a hang glider and flew it in the cow pastures of what would later become the North Hills neighborhood in Bedford, VA
- Killed a copperhead snake with an ice pick (protecting daughter and grandchild)
- Jumped into an 8-foot sink hole to rescue daughter's Sheltie
- Rescued a 5-year-old boy who fell in water between a dock and a boat at a Marina in Myrtle Beach
- Saved a student's life who cut an artery when his arm when through

a window
- Had one of the highest SOL World History student pass rates in the district
- Sang "Silent Night" in German each Christmas
- Built a fallout shelter made out of cinder blocks in my house in Western Hills in the 1960s (learned this in a civil defense class that teachers were required to take)
- In a Hampden-Sydney dorm walked up a flight of stairs and down a hall on my hands
- Nickname, "Golden Toe Cutler," kicker on Richlands High School Football Team
- Legal name, Joseph Holden Cutler, Jr.

Acknowledgments

I would like to thank all those who made my dream of sharing some stories in a book a reality. These include:

- My daughter, Dr. Cherie Cutler Whitehurst, who typed my writing and oral dictation, and helped me with this project from beginning to end.
- Retired Lt. Commander Navy SEAL Ed Hiner for writing the Preface and front cover blurb and for his lifetime encouragement and support.
- Special thanks to Rick Peterson, Pitching Coach of the *Moneyball* Oakland A's, for the back cover blurb and for offering to call me on the phone for a chat.
- Mark Damon Puckett for his excellent work as editor and publisher at Onion Scribe Publishing in Fairfield, Connecticut.
- My son-in-law David Whitehurst and his sister Monica Whitehurst for proofreading.
- My sons, Mike, Ken, and Jeff, and friend Harold Jones, for providing feedback.
- For typing and proofreading, much gratitude also goes to my granddaughter Anne Cantrell and her husband Henry, as well as to my granddaughter Dr. Alison Martin and her husband Alex.
- I want to deeply thank Ann Jackson for giving me permission to use Zim's artwork of my image on the front cover.
- Mitchell Bond of Goose Creek Studio scanned and digitized Zim Jackson's art under a deadline and I want to thank him too for doing this so quickly.

- Lori Mattson, Liberty High School Athletic Director, and Brian Sennett, Liberty High School Athletic Trainer, helped with photography for my author photo. Many thanks!

And of course, I want to thank all my family and friends for their encouragement and support on this project.

And finally, I want to thank God for His many wonderful blessings in my life.